I0140470

Garden
of
Light

Aligning with
Your True Nature

And Receiving Inner Guidance

Karen McChrystal, MA

Garden of Light:

Aligning with Your True Nature and Receiving Inner Guidance

Copyright © 2011, 2016
by Karen McChrystal

All rights reserved, including the right to reproduce this work in any form whatsoever, without permission in writing from the author, except for brief passages in connection with a review.

ISBN: 978-0-9973842-0-8

Cover design by Suzanne Burgos
Editing by Lynn Thomas
Back cover photo by Jon Matlick

Warm Springs Press
Tucson, Arizona

To the people who have understood what I've tried to do
in this book and supported me in the endeavor,
to those who contributed with comments and editing;
and to like-minded individuals who have been there giving moral
support from their own
non-ordinary ways of knowing.
Thank you all!

CONTENTS

Preface

Garden of Light was written to share with you a vision and a way to envision a positive path to the future. Individually, this path can be one of peacefulness and fulfillment, even in the midst of great uncertainty and chaos in the surrounding world resulting from the unwinding of the old system. Collectively, it can be a path to the creation and unfurling of a future that likely will look and feel considerably different from the present, and the past several generations.

What is needed now is a view that is transcendent, and one that integrates psychological, spiritual, scientific and practical understanding. In my experience, it is important to have a clarified inner life, in order to clearly perceive the bigger picture and to guide one's understanding in other aspects of reality. Cultivating the inner life – cultivating the garden within – gets one back to one's true nature and the ability to live authentically. One may also receive Inner Guidance and inspiration to fuel creativity, not only to live from a creative spirit, but also to make positive contributions to the vast transformative process now ensuing in our world.

This book is a practical guide to finding one's way toward fulfillment and even enlightenment. The more one identifies and clarifies the Self, the more enlightened one becomes. Enlightenment – "bringing in light" – invites greater awareness of, and appreciation for the All That Is.

Over the past twenty years, by developing and deepening my connection with Inner Guidance, I have received immeasurable help both in navigating through perilous times, as well as in personal endeavors. While enduring health and financial crises, which happened early in my life, I learned that Inner Guidance is always present, always forthcoming. At the same time, I have been supported, even pushed by Inner Guidance, to continue learning and to keep my mind and skills fresh and sharp.

This book shares my vision of how non-ordinary ways of knowing, when combined with ordinary comprehension, inspiration and creativity, can very effectively contribute to the creation of a better world. The text recounts my personal journey, combined with my version of the "big picture." I have also included contributions from other visionary thinkers whose ideas concur with mine and whom I believe are well worth knowing about, each with their special focus. The second half of the book is practical and highlights areas that I believe need to be included in our understanding and actions. This is so that our futures, individually and collectively, can be wisely charted and more positively and productively lived.

~ Karen McChrystal, MA, 2016

Chapter 1.

The Garden as a Classroom

One often takes an unexpected turn in the never-ending quest to live a deeply satisfying and meaningful life. In my late forties, I experienced just such a turn. Suddenly I was able to tune in to other dimensions – beyond my five senses. At the same time, I discovered I could receive extremely clear messages from Inner Guidance in the form of words and images. This happened at a time when the meaning in my work as a psychotherapist had completely dissipated. After thirteen years practicing in this field I was no longer gaining any satisfaction from the work, nor was I learning or growing. In fact, I was feeling downright depressed in the process.

While psychotherapy is a fine and noble profession, I had never felt it was my true calling, even though I was good at it. Now finally it was time for me to grow in other ways and experience new things. I quit my successful practice, much to the dismay of my then-husband.

I was faced then with daunting question of what I really wanted to do. To help clear my mind I turned to nature. Behind our home in Fairfax, California there was an expanse of uncultivated land, open space, which I thought could be turned into a garden. For a few hours each day, while mulling over what steps to take next professionally, I gardened. This proved extremely therapeutic. Having my hands in the soil seemed to ground and return me to my own nature. I found myself "recovering" from my work as a psychotherapist, letting go of the emotional and mental weight of all those I'd carried in my practice. This contact with nature re-charged me. In my little garden, I began opening to new dimensions....

The Foxes

Behind our home, in the open space adjacent to our property stood a sixty-foot high prehistoric rock formation. Atop this rock are three Miwok Indian grinding bowls – deep impressions worn into the rock from years of grinding acorns and other grains on its surface. A wooded area surrounded this formation, filled by bay laurel, eucalyptus, madrone and acacia trees. From the top of the rock one could see Mt. Tamalpais, the highest mountain in Marin County, known as "The Sleeping Lady." The enclosed valley stretching from the base of the rock is reputed to have been the site of a Miwok village before white men burned it to the ground two centuries ago. My Native-American Indian medicine woman friend, whom I'll call Rayanne, who possessed the ability to see spirits, assured me that Indian spirits still hovered around the rock, and that it served as a sacred altar for women's medicine. According to Rayanne, the grinding bowls were used exclusively by the women of the tribe to grind medicinal herbs, acorns and grains for food.

Whenever I sat on top of the rock, a powerful energy surged through my body. I was sitting there one day when the foxes first appeared. I had been meditating with my eyes closed. On opening them, I found myself staring directly into the eyes of a fox sitting fifteen feet away, peering across at me from among the bushes. We contemplated each other for several minutes before he ran up the trail and barked to another fox somewhere behind the rock ridge.

Two days later, when out watering plants on the patio beside the house, I heard what sounded like a raven cawing nearby – a raspy barking sound. When I scanned the wooded slope behind the patio, I saw a fox sitting about twenty feet away, looking right at me. It was the fox that was barking at me! He (or she) sat upright, with his forelegs delicately positioned, the way a cat sits. As I had been in the habit of meowing back at our neighbor's cat that "talked" incessantly, it seemed only natural to bark back at the fox. He cocked his head, then barked back. Our interspecies "conversation" lasted about ten minutes. Suddenly a second fox appeared and joined in the conversation. I had no idea what our barks were conveying, but evidently the exchange was meaningful, for the foxes upheld their end of the conversation.

After another ten minutes of barking at each other we went our separate ways. I was deeply affected by the experience. I remembered stories told about the Indian mystic Ramana Maharshi, who strolled with wild animals peacefully walking beside him. Jokingly I told friends I wasn't sufficiently enlightened for the foxes to come sit in my lap. Still, I did not really understand the deeper meaning of our exchange. This I did know: I had become more peaceful since leaving my practice. Were the foxes simply sensing that peacefulness, and feeling safe being near me? I also had been meditating fairly regularly. Had I become more enlightened, due to inner work? Was I now more "full of light," or more "in the light" such that the foxes would deign to communicate with me? Were they telling me we shared a connection? To this day, I still have no answers. Nevertheless, I felt thrilled to have been "contacted" by them, and to watch the gap narrow between me and the little foxes.

The Deer

We shared the space behind our home with the original inhabitants – many, many deer. They roamed freely and frequently, often coming to within a foot of the back of our house. Our property was demarcated from the surrounding open space by a single row of two-by-ten-inch wooden planks set horizontally along the perimeter. This proved no impediment to the deer, who regularly leapt five-foot fences into the neighbors' yards.

Naively, I assumed I could plant flowers around the patio, thinking the deer would not be so brazen as to venture into an exposed area next to the back door and visible from kitchen windows. So thinking, I brought back from the nursery various flowering plants and some plants for ground cover. These I planted along the border of the patio. Apparently the deer assumed I had put the plants there for them, for within twenty minutes after I had retreated indoors not a petal or leaf remained. Every flower, every plant, had been nibbled down to stubs. Disappointed though I was, I tried again, this time planting what the nurseryman said were tougher, leafier "deer resistant" plants. Alas, the deer loved these too, and signaled their pleasure by depositing little brown calling cards amidst the stubble as thanks for the feast. Obviously, the deer owned the place, so this time I gave up.

Shortly thereafter, one afternoon as I was resting, I drifted into a hypnogogic state of half-sleep. An image of the face of a deer – a buck – looking right at me, came to my mind's eye (that space inside your head you see when you close your eyes). My first reaction was to feel mildly angry and resentful toward the deer for eating my plants. Noting this, I decided to change my attitude from adversarial to amicable. Perhaps, I told myself, I could persuade the deer to stop eating my garden! It seemed worth a try.

After clearing my inner hostility I summoned up some love for the deer. As soon as that happened, the expression on the buck's face changed from fear to openness. I proceeded mentally to tell him I wanted him and his friends to remove my garden from their dinner menu. I explained I wanted to help Mother Nature, to learn how to grow things, to create a place of beauty, and to teach what I learned about our connection with nature. Sensing I needed to give something back, I told him the deer were welcome to eat the agapanthuses in our front yard. I knew deer were particularly fond of agapanthus flower buds, having seen them repeatedly nip the buds. Because our yard contained the only source on the block, I assumed I had some good leverage. I gathered that the deer spirit understood and even agreed with the bargain because, during the course of our conversation while looking right at me, the expression in his eyes became increasingly peaceful.

The next day, I had another try at gardening. I replaced little flowering plants – genuine deer delicacies – and watched to see if they would be eaten. Days passed, then weeks. The flowers remained and the plants grew healthy, mature and strong. From our bedroom window I watched the deer pass behind the garden perimeter five or six times a day on their foraging runs. They consistently ignored my plants! Emboldened by this, I planted a larger area in the back yard, again with tender flowering plants that no one else in the neighborhood dared plant. Those plants survived too! Meanwhile, the agapanthus buds in the front yard were devoured. As well, each agapanthus leaf had one little deer bite removed from its tip – a raggedy sight, but well worth the trade-off.

In a second mind's eye conversation with the deer spirit, I made sure to thank him. Years later, after I had moved away, I heard that the deer had started eating the back yard garden plants again. Apparently I had to be there.

From this experience I learned that the entire spirit realm is not some other-worldly place inhabited angels and dead saints (not that I'd ever quite believed in that concept). If deer could respect my desire to grow a garden for my own learning, they must be connected with a reality larger than their immediate need to survive. I don't know what they understood, exactly, but I felt supported by them in allowing me to cultivate my garden. More important to me, though, was the evidence I gained that Spirit is part of our lives and must, in some ways, connect us all.

The Elements

One afternoon as I lay resting, looking out my back window at the big rock, I drifted into a meditative semi-trance state once again. Into my mind's eye came a progression of images of the molecular structures of different elements. First to appear was a substance that seemed to be sulphur – a sphere defined by yellow lines circling it. I sensed it was showing me in the properties of sulphur, which seemed to be a form-holding element.

Next came an image of what I intuited was phosphorus – feathery-like branches arching upward, like marsh rushes. The branches were reddish in color and emitted a soft reddish glow. The image conveyed that in essence phosphorus is a heat giver. Next I saw blue-silver crystals of a metallic element. While it resembled hematite or magnetite, in fact it was iron. From the image I understood that iron, in its metallic form, has weight and coolness.

Next an image appeared of the delicate yellow buttercup I had planted days before next to some ochre-colored phosphorus-bearing rocks. The buttercup had not been doing well. In fact, it was a bit droopy. Now in my mind's eye, its leaves appeared brown and crisp, its roots shriveled. The plant was burning up from being too close to the phosphorus rocks. While phosphorus is required by all plants, including buttercups, the image suggested that this delicate little plant was absorbing too much.

Though these were merely visions, unsupported by objective scientific research, I was sufficiently intrigued to test their merit by experimenting in my garden. (In a laboratory it could probably be demonstrated that rocks with crystalline structures can pick up electro-magnetic waves from the atmosphere, modulate and transmit them in a manner similar to how a crystal radio set detects radio waves, modulates and transmits them. Crystal radios can receive weak signals without using amplification.)

I moved the buttercups; I planted them and other delicate plants away from the phosphorus-bearing rocks, and placed the woodier plants that benefit from more phosphorus closer to these hot rocks. This produced positive results: the plants thrived.

I learned more about minerals in rocks, seeing images in my mind's eye which told me which plants needed to be near which rocks to provide the frequency of specific mineral or trace elements they required. Guided by the imagery I was receiving I experimented with placing certain small rocks near specific plants. Judging from the results, this worked well too. Overnight a droopy or pale plant would revive after being placed next to the rock(s) containing the mineral element it needed. I also looked into my mind's eye to receive images about which plant food or how much water to give each plant. My plants simply thrived!

Parable of the Aphids

Above and beyond learning about the spirit interconnectedness of all beings in nature, I also was given a lesson in how this connection goes even further! One early spring morning in Fairfax, I happened to look closely at the rose bush that scaled the two stories and spilled over onto the roof of my home. It was in full bloom, covered with hundreds of small white roses. To my dismay, the stems and tender new leaves were thickly covered with aphids – billions of tiny green sucking machines, sucking the life out of my beloved climbing rose. Appalled though I was, I would not use insecticide, which poisons far more than just the intended insect targets. Instead, I said an earnest prayer to the Almighty that a new home be found for the aphids. After all, the property bordered on open space with miles of wild vegetation for the aphids to eat.

The next morning, to my great surprise and delight, nary an aphid was to be seen! Feeling elated and grateful, I set out on my morning walk to a sewing notions store on the main street of our small town. Inside, a small group of women were gathered around at the counter talking about God, interestingly enough! One said that God didn't have time or care for her small concerns. I responded by telling the aphid story, and concluded by saying that if God could take care of these tiny little bugs, why not each of us?

Perhaps the aphids left all at once for some other reason than prayer, but I can't fathom what that other reason might be. I'm happy to report, however, that they had not drained the rose bush of all its spring juices; there were new shoots appearing daily, and the rose bush survived and thrived.

My gardening project gave me far more than I had expected at the start. The little garden became my classroom. Here I learned about my connection with nature. For me, the garden was a sacred space. Each time I entered, I left my cares behind and was embraced by the rich stillness and goodness of nature. The soil itself reconnected me with my deepest self. The more in tune with nature I became, the more I felt nature support the rhythms and harmonies of my innermost being. To this day, I continue to "tune in" to spirit, to directly sense what my plants need.

I had always been quite sensitive. As a very young child I had been able to sense subtleties that those around me seemed either not to be aware of, or to ignore. I would "know" things, or feel things, almost to the point of being clairsentient. My parents denied my perceptions. They told me I could not be feeling what I described, or that I was too sensitive, or that I could not possibly know the information I was sharing. Perhaps this sensitivity demonstrated an awareness of spiritual dimensions *per se*. I don't know. Having been invalidated as far as my intuitions and subtle perceptions, throughout my early adulthood I felt compelled to develop my skills in logic and scholarship so I could to "prove" to others that what I understood was verifiable.

Even so, I largely ignored my own intuitions and became a staunch atheist, for a number of reasons. I remained such until my mid-thirties, when I experienced a re-opening of my spirituality. I did not attempt, at this point (or at any point thereafter), to align with any specific religion. I preferred instead to understand through my own experience, realities beyond that which we can experience with our five senses or measure with science. Zen Buddhism did appeal to me, though, for its bare bones un-ornamented perspective.

The spiritual re-awakening came in the process of my learning a powerful method of using the breath. This will be explored later in the book, but for now, suffice it to say that during one of these "breath sessions" I experienced being enfolded in an effulgent, brilliant, yet soft light that filled me with profound feelings of peace and joy and the sense of being held by a great benevolent Presence. Following that, I no longer chose to deny the existence of God, though I didn't conclude much more than that at the time.

I continued seeking, learning from excellent teachers and studying books on mysticism and Zen Buddhism. At the time, I was practicing as a psychotherapist. As is recommended for all therapists, I also went through my own psychotherapy. I mention this because my understanding as I set forth in these pages has not come easily. I am not proffering any quick fixes or instant formulas for having a miraculous life.

I continued working with the breath. Recognizing its power to help people access deeper understandings within themselves, I taught the method, and continued to learn from my breath teacher, Maurice Rowdon (now deceased). His background was in pranayama yoga, and the teachings of Ramana Maharshi and Paramahansa Yogananda.

Then in my early forties I experienced a severe health crisis, caused mostly by physical depletion and toxicities. Traditional MDs and alternative health practitioners were unable to help. This led me finally to a woman healer who returned me to perfect health, a condition which has lasted for the past fifteen years, in which state I've remained ever since. In fact, I have not been sick for even one day.

Before I'd met her, this healer, in the course of her own serious health crisis, had had a near death experience. When she came back to life, after being clinically dead for seven minutes, she had gained the ability to tune in to the dimension of Spirit and to hear an audible voice, which identified itself as the Creator. Thenceforth, she received very detailed Inner Guidance, in the form of words, daily, for the rest of her life. She used this Guidance to heal others from all kinds of ailments, including schizophrenia, blindness, Parkinson's, cancer and lupus – everything short of Lou Gehrig's disease. It took four years for her to restore me to perfect health. The way she did it was by prescribing herbal and nutritional remedies according to guidance she "received" from Spirit, or God. As important, it was she who taught me how to tune in to the dimension of Spirit and receive my own Inner Guidance.

Tuning in to Inner Guidance hardly came naturally for me, for two reasons: I have a very active mental life, and I like to feel in control. So the essential stillness and surrender took time for me to learn. I already had prepared myself for this experience to a large extent, by my earlier studies with superb teachers and good books, and through my knowledge of psychology and psychotherapy. But the most important part was learning to clear and quiet my mind so that I could distinguish my own thoughts, analysis, judgment, skepticism and imagination from that which was coming from beyond. Once I learned to "tune in," and was able to verify what I was receiving enough to trust it, I understood that this was something nearly anyone can do if they believe it is possible and if they do their inner work. That said, it still took me a few years to undo my own disbelief. Hopefully the recounting of my experience will save you some time.

My personal strong suits are in language and intuition. Given this, most of what I receive from Spirit, or Inner Guidance, comes in the form of words. They are quite distinct from my own thoughts. The best way I've found to describe it is they're like words of air.

When I first started receiving messages from Inner Guidance, I used a method I'd learned to test the source and accuracy of the messages. This (physician-approved) method, kinesiology, also known as "muscle testing," directly reflects the state of the body-mind. Strong muscle strength indicates a "yes" or "this is good for you" answer, whereas weak muscles indicate "false," or "not good for you." I ran hundreds of tests before I gained total confidence in my ability to receive accurate information. After a few months of dedicated attention to "receiving," my clairvoyance ("clear seeing") and clairsentience ("clear feeling") became stronger and more reliable. Now I can receive reliable Inner Guidance as words, images, a strongly "felt sense," and sometimes as an undeniable "knowingness."

Why would one choose to develop these abilities? For myself, I had a successful career, a solid income, an intelligent, gentle and kind husband, yet my life lacked a certain something. I was greatly impressed by the healer's ability to "prescribe" remedies," through her Inner Guidance, and this entirely over the telephone. The physical healing followed a precise order, taking into account not only what toxicities had to be cleansed in what order, but also which organs had to be healed in which order. She was able to give me an instant diagnosis of whatever was needed at the moment, the exact remedies and precise amounts of supplement, herb or food to take. My then-husband also received healing work from her.

The healer's unerring ability to receive such accurate and effective information for my healing convinced me of the presence of Divine Intelligence. It is possible that a very skilled medical intuitive could have done the same thing, but I'd be surprised. In any case, I very much wanted to learn for myself how to do this. I wanted to have a direct connection with the Creator! (Hereafter, references to God will be interchangeable in hopes that one feels comfortable to you, the reader: Source, God, All That Is, Supreme Being... I don't think the term matters so much.)

Being a scholar, and ever hungry for deeper understanding and knowledge, the act of connecting with a Being that exists beyond the known realm and receiving answers to any and all questions was the *piece de resistance*. Once gaining the ability to receive Inner Guidance, I used it in every aspect of my life. I received answers to questions when answers could not be found through ordinary means. I asked the "big questions" about life, about what really happened in various historically recorded events, about physics, about ascension, about the nature of the soul and what happens to it after death, about the functions of higher beings in the firmament… anything and everything I was puzzled about. And I got answers! I received Guidance for solving problems of all sorts, directions for finding whatever material object I needed, such as an article of clothing, or a book containing information I was seeking, or what food or nutritional supplements I needed at any given time….

To receive answers from Inner Guidance, one must first ask the question. In this regard, I'm reminded of a story told to me by a former colleague, a devout Catholic whom I'll call William. One day William made up his mind he wanted to hear from God, to have some proof of His existence. He went to the church chapel alone on a day when it was otherwise empty. Sitting in the pew, he firmly asked God to speak to him. Then he waited. And waited. Finally he heard the clear reply, "I'm waiting, William. Don't waste my time. What is the question?"

Since I first began to use Inner Guidance, its role in my life has expanded. As my knowledge and access deepens, I have more advanced questions to ask, as well the ongoing more mundane questions. Increasingly I find myself "being moved" to do the right and appropriate thing. I "know" the answers almost as soon as I pose the question. I have learned through my reading that people on a sincere spiritual path gain ever greater access to the All That Is.

Relying on Inner Guidance does not mean we stop using our brains and common sense. Nor does it mean ignoring information available through ordinary means. You must do the homework, learn what you can from available sources, remain alert, aware and discerning. After that, after doing your homework, you can receive more help from Divine Guidance. In this way, life becomes a co-creative adventure!

Inner Guidance is often called the "still, small voice" because it can only be heard when one's mind is still. The voice is "small" compared with our normal thoughts. Inner Guidance should never be used to tell others what to do. It does not urge us to seek power and domination over others, to go to war, to launch self-righteous crusades. To be truly guided, our motives must be pure; ego needs must be set aside. We must assume an attitude of surrender.

For those called to walk the spiritual path, receiving guidance from Source is invaluable. It quickens one's spiritual progress and makes life easier in many ways. Becoming aware of the spiritual dimension in all things is revolutionary in that it overturns all notions of reality as being limited to the physical world and its dynamics. Awareness of the spirit in all beings and things opens up a world of infinite possibilities.

"Trying to deny the existence of God

is like telling a snail to go faster."

CHAPTER 2.

THE GARDEN OF BEING

The cultivation of a garden can be seen as a metaphor for the cultivation of self. Nature's laws form a subset of physical laws, and contains a wild card: biological nature. Biology is complex. Its organic chemistry can, with great difficulty, be described in formulas, but it is easier to understand nature as being a complex response to a complex set of circumstances or environment. And so, to live fully in accordance with our own nature and come into our full potential, we need to have some understanding of our biology as well as our complex responses to the environment.

Being true to one's nature means being true to one's innate design for coming into health, wholeness and full potential. Cultivating the garden of one's being is a relatively simple analogy, but I think appropriate. A garden environment can be healthy and flourish or it can be harmed by predatory insect pests, inadequate nutrients, improper soil, lack of water, climate, and manmade poisons, such as pesticides.

All biological life is flexible and adaptable, but perhaps not as capable of assuming as many forms as can human beings. Human nature is protean: mutable, capable of assuming many forms, flexible, versatile and adaptable. This protean nature of man has left many people endlessly debating the question of what is human nature. I believe it worthwhile to consider that one can distinguish between a false and a true nature. Our true nature is what we experience when we are true to the whole of our Self. Aligning with our true nature leads us in the direction of increasing levels of fulfillment, and ultimately to enlightenment.

If we wish to experience our own true nature and thus unfold the full potential of being, we should think first of weeding the garden of our psyche. Spiritual growth comes from the deepest part of ourselves. We need to get at the root of any discomforts we may have, and "uproot" them, in order to create peacefulness in the ground of our being and to connect with our true spirituality – our experience of Oneness. This is not a purely mental activity; it involves our emotional aspects as well. It begins with understanding where we come from and what has made us who we are today, on the emotional as well as the intellectual level.

Some people try to improve their lives by repeating positive affirmations or mantras over and over. But the beneficial effects of these, if any, are usually short-lived. If we unconsciously hold onto and believe in our psychological "weeds," such as believing we are unimportant, undeserving or limited, affirmations can do no more than temporarily short-circuit our belief. Telling ourselves everything will work out for the best does no good if we don't really believe it, consciously and unconsciously.

Our inner life determines what we allow ourselves to have, to aspire to, and how we behave and what we learn. If, for instance, we want to be more successful in our career but we secretly believe we don't deserve success, we'll unconsciously sabotage our efforts in order to conform to our unconscious beliefs. Conversely, if we believe we're truly deserving, we'll draw to ourselves the people and situations that help us. *[author's note: pop psychology uses the term "subconscious," but I prefer to stick to the strict Freudian terminology, which uses the categories of unconscious and pre-conscious. The unconscious, according to the Freudians, is where lie the roots of buried pathogenic beliefs.]*

Weeding the Garden

Weeding our psychological garden means identifying whatever is in our psyche that is unbeautiful, (i.e., pathogenic beliefs) and uprooting them. In the psyche, however, the pathogenic thought, belief or attitude may be rooted very deeply in our unconscious mind, where lie its childhood origins. And so understanding where we came from, what has shaped us, is important if we are to transcend our conditioning.

As we weed our inner garden, more light comes into it, without the shadows cast by the weeds… we have less confusion and therefore more clarity, more light. Our inner garden and our outer world become more beautiful. As within, so without. If we harbor negative thought patterns, we see our negativity reflected in the world around us. But if we dismantle them, we see the beauty and possibilities which surround us. This process enables us to become more open, and new perceptions become possible. And by and by, we become able to perceive more subtle aspects of the nature around us and of our own nature.

Cultivating Inner Peacefulness

From the space of inner peacefulness can arise insights and resolutions to problems and troublesome thought patterns. Insight can arise automatically, given that the human psyche has embedded in it its own inner design and plan for healing* and the unconscious mind, via the pre-conscious, can send us messages in our mind's eye (in addition to messages in our dreams). (*Weiss and Sampson, 1986)

Although the human psyche has an innate plan for healing, there are, of course, people who are very stuck, and ever so many who have never sat still long enough to "get to the bottom of things," so to speak. It is not sufficient to simply re-experience an old feeling and leave it at that. Many psychotherapies fail because the unskilled therapist does allow the patient to stop at that. Thoughts that are self-destructive must be dismantled, to free one to have a healthy response, and painful emotion must be worked through until one returns to a state of equanimity.

Most commonly, people carry around old baggage from childhood trauma, which caused the child to be worried about his or her survival or well-being. Based on the child's interpretation of reality as to why the traumatic event occurred, he will have formed unconscious theories – pathogenic beliefs – about his own defenselessness, unworthiness, or undeservingness. This is not to suggest that the child's experience and the conclusions he or she draws from traumatic events are invalid. The issue is that once the child becomes an adult, he or she need not continue having expectations that what happened in childhood will continue to happen. False Expectations Appearing Real = FEAR.

As psychologist Dr. George Silberschatz, of the Mt. Zion Psychotherapy Research Group, explains,

> "Children develop theories as part of their efforts to cope with trauma, and in their theorizing they are prone to draw irrational conclusions, which typically lead to self-blame and guilt. Harold Weiss termed these theories 'pathogenic beliefs' and argued that such beliefs are the cornerstone of later psychopathology. For example: a child who had been mistreated by her parents developed the pathogenic belief that she deserved mistreatment. That unconscious belief led to psychopathology later in her life, including depression, disturbed relationships, and substance abuse." (Silberschatz 2008)

It isn't a simple matter, usually, to deconstruct self-destructive thought patterns or to work through painful emotions. Most people will benefit from the help of a trained psychotherapist to do this work. A good therapist is one who has accurate empathy. By that I mean, you must get the feeling that the therapist understands you and understands what you're trying to achieve in life, what your goals are, as far as your personal development.

I still remember the thing that made me end my sessions with one of my own psychotherapists. After I'd been seeing this particular therapist for about three months, he stated that he thought I'd make a good hospital administrator. Talk about inaccurate empathy! I could hardly imagine a more unpleasant job for myself. The thought of doing paperwork, directing the finances and overall performance of a medical institution, when I thought in any case that traditional American medicine was horrible, often criminal, was about the last thing I wanted to do!

A good therapist must also be skilled enough to have insight into what the issues are that are holding you back or that are painful for you and will will know how to get at the deeper underlying causes. The therapist also acts like a mirror for us, when we are unable to see ourselves, especially when unconscious issues are holding us back. Talk therapy can be supplemented with clinical hypnosis or guided imagery work.

Pop psychology is full of talk about overcoming feelings of unworthiness that come from a parent having been harsh, abusive, cold, or critical. Something pop psychology, including so-called "life coaching," usually doesn't get at is how brilliant the patient is at working, in his therapy (and in close personal relationships), to disprove his pathogenic beliefs, according to his unconscious plan for getting better. When the patient is allowed to pursue his own treatment agenda, he or she works hard in order to disprove his pathogenic beliefs.

Nor does pop psychology talk about guilt-based fear of success, which is a fear of succeeding because to do so would make a parent (or peer, upon whom one depends) feel outdone or small by comparison. Or that caretaker is needy and doesn't want the child to succeed on his or her own terms and live a life of his own, away from the caretaker. So the adult carries around guilt about "abandoning" the parent, and self-sabotages, especially whenever he or she is right on the verge of succeeding.

Two other self-inhibiting patterns overlooked by pop psychology are "identification" and what is called "passive into active." Identification is when an individual unconsciously identifies with a parent, adopting an artificial personality that hides and inhibits who that individual really is. "Passive into active" is when an individual does to another what was done to them by an abusive parent or captor. Both of these patterns are enacted unconsciously; both prevent the individual from fully maturing and living authentically.

There is much research and volumes of case studies giving ample evidence that the patient has a plan, albeit usually unconscious, to get better. The unconscious mind is untiring and highly intelligent in trying to find ways for the individual to heal. (Weiss and Sampson 1986) This research and case studies come out of the Mt. Zion Psychotherapy Research Institute, in San Francisco. The model is known as the "Control Mastery Theory." In my own private practice as a psychotherapist, I employed the Control Mastery treatment model with great success. This, along with clinical hypnosis was by far the most effective of the various therapy modalities I used with my clients.

To summarize, undoing pathogenic beliefs takes some work, because they're tangled up in our child's reasoning and usually buried in our unconscious mind. We first need to become aware of the beliefs themselves, track the beliefs back to their origins, usually in childhood, and finally understand that what may have happened then or what may have been required of us in order to survive, physically and/or emotionally need not happen again. It is essential that we feel safe in the present before we allow ourselves to re-visit an old trauma; otherwise, we're frozen in a defensive attitude. If we have no "safe harbor" but instead are in the company of people who do the same traumatizing things to us, then we can't heal. There is no substitute for the "corrective experience" of relating to people who treat us with love and respect. That person can be a therapist and/or a close friend or relative.

Being Healthy in a Sick Society

One can be psychologically healthy, even when living in a sick society such as our own in the United States. Psychological health is being able to respond appropriately and effectively to our circumstances. Anxiety and fear keep us off-balance, reacting defensively. Whether through psychotherapy, meditation, or both, the most important thing is to be able to stay in peacefulness no matter what. Coming from a place of peacefulness allows us to give the most effective responses to any affronts or abuses, or to determine the best ways to surmount obstacles.

In our day-to-day life, taking time for quiet reflection allows us to come up with clear analysis and effective approaches for confronting wrong-doing, for standing up for ourselves. For example, while feeling anger is not in itself unhealthy, and is often quite a healthy response to social and personal injustices and cruelties, what is important is how we express the anger. Time spent in reflection can help us arrive at a problem-solving, well-considered tactical approach. This is far healthier and more effective than simply venting one's anger or returning attack for attack.

The Persistent Ego

The ego is a very tricky character. It can present us with all sorts of ideas that have the persuasiveness of a major ad agency. It may cater to our self-satisfaction or desire for something harmful or essentially irrelevant to our lives. The seductions of ego can be persistent, even when we're fairly advanced in our spiritual development. If not kept in its proper place, ego asserts its own agenda. It may even take on a life of its own, as though it were our ship's captain, giving directions and pretending to know everything.

Ego isn't supposed to be in the captain's seat. If given too much power, it goes its own way, often oblivious to consequences. The qualities of ego are not our best qualities. Ego can be brash, insensitive, superior, shallow, insincere, reckless, grandiose or demanding. It hurts others and justifies the act. It pretends not to see the suffering it causes. Ego passes the buck.

The goal is not to abolish the ego, but to keep it in its place. The word ego is Latin for "I," or the first person singular. From the clinical point of view, the term ego refers to a part of our psychology which we need – the interface between our individual consciousness and society. The healthy ego mediates between desire (the id and the pleasure principle), the super-ego, and external reality. As Sigmund Freud wrote in *An Outline of Psychoanalysis,*

> On behalf of the id, the ego controls the path of access to motility, but it interpolates between desire and action the procrastinating factor of thought, during which it makes use of the residues of experience stored up in memory. In this way it dethrones the pleasure-principle, which exerts undisputed sway over the processes in the id, and substitutes for it the reality-principle, which promises greater security and greater success. (Freud 1940)

To put it simply, the ego is the coherent organization of mental processes. (Freud 1923) The healthy ego is what gives us the ability to stand up for our individuality. Ego, here, is like a transparent envelope that contains our individualized self. It speaks rationally for our inner being so that we can effectively be seen and heard for who we really are, in the outer world. Healthy ego in this sense enables us to say, rationally, what we really think, feel or need.

Egotism is different from ego as healthy individuality. For example, I may become an authority on Impressionist Art. I tell myself the reason is because Impressionism teaches so much about aesthetics, color and light. But I become very involved in my expert knowledge and make others feel ignorant about the subject so that I can feel important. This is egotism – a device to help us build up our sense of worth at the expense of others. This may go in the right direction, and we may need to act this way for a time to feel good about ourselves. But a better way would be to discover why we feel bad about ourselves in the first place. Once we've reassured ourselves that we're essentially important, we can give up our posture of superiority, still knowing our worth. We can let go of our defensive bit of identity.

Some people equate all forms of ego to selfishness, including individuality. So they counter this by being altruistic – giving without regard for their own needs. This adaptation is based on a misunderstanding. Selfishness in the negative sense is taking care of one's self without respect for others and our environment. Taking care of one's self without taking advantage of others, however, is selfishness in a positive sense, in the sense of standing up for one's Self and for what one truly needs and believes as one's truth. If we don't take care of ourselves, in this sense, we won't have anything to give to others. Think about it … If you altruistically give all your money to homeless people, you'll end up homeless too. And how much would you really have helped the homeless? Mother Teresa didn't give it all away – she always had a convent in which to live.

Some people join cults that insist all ego is bad. The cult leader demands that individuality be submerged in the collective consciousness of the group, which usually means in the consciousness of the group leader. Cults are very seductive for people who long for love and acceptance so much they'll give up their individuality for it. Many who join cults are looking for a stand-in mother or father figure to make up for what they missed growing up. The group's offer of what appears to be unconditional love and acceptance, however, soon turns sour, as the leader usually feeds his own ego from the subservience of his acolytes. A true spiritual leader encourages his students to develop their own insights and abilities, not to become unquestioning followers.

Cultivating the garden of our soul, attending to our inner life, reconnects us to our innate design for healing, for personal evolution to fuller and fuller potential, and for being able to receive Inner Guidance. Once the baseline of psychological health has been achieved, and we are in touch with our inner guidance, we are then prepared to open to other dimensions, which can be incorporated as a next stage in our personal evolution. The All That Is is eternally present. Being able to remain aware of the Eternal Present while at the same time living in a relative world is the challenge and the goal.

CHAPTER 3.

MEDITATION

Outside of being in psychotherapeutic treatment, meditation can be used to advantage to understand our inner psychology. Sitting meditation will serve the purpose, if we do it in a disciplined way, i.e., for long enough periods and with enough regularity. Begin by sitting daily, doing nothing, just observing your thoughts. Don't get caught up in them; just watch them go by like so many passing clouds. The beginning meditator at first usually finds there is so much clamor in his or her mind that it will be difficult to just sit and trust that the clamor will quiet down. Resist efforts to jump up and get "busy." Just keep sitting. This will eventually take you to a point where the mind chatter stops and you're moving into deeper and deeper levels of peacefulness. When your mind is quiet and you feel peaceful, your mind's eye can reveal to you what your deeper mind believes or needs to reveal to you. Peacefulness gives you the objectivity and insight needed to achieve clarity.

However vast outer space may be, yet with all its sidereal distances it hardly bears comparison with the dimensions, with the depth dimension of our inner being, which does not even need the spaciousness of the universe to be within itself almost unfathomable...

~ Rainer Maria Rilke

Summary of the Benefits of Meditation

The primary benefits gained from regular meditation are these:

- You'll get in touch with who you really are – your authentic self, what you really think, feel and want for yourself.

- You'll begin to understand what your life purpose is.

- By focusing and aligning with who you truly are, you'll attract into your life everything you need to evolve and be fulfilled.

- You'll be able to respond spontaneously and appropriately to any situation.

- You'll develop greater adaptability.

- You'll gain more clarity and focus.

- You'll more easily be proactive, thereby realizing your dreams and goals.

- Your efficiency increases, and you will have ease in doing whatever you want to do.

- Your body will be able to heal itself and maintain health and resistance to disease.

🐾 Your intelligence increases. As do some contemplative practices, prayer, and breathwork, meditation actually changes your brain.

🐾 You experience more joyfulness, love and compassion.

🐾 As your practice deepens, you are able to access the infinite mind, the Quantum Field, God, or whatever you call it.

🐾 As you progress further you'll begin receiving higher energies from the Divine Source.

Belly Breathing: Accelerated Meditation

One can accelerate the meditative process of quieting the mind and going into a deep peaceful state, beneath the clamorous level of daily preoccupations and concerns. This is done by using certain breathing methods. The best method I've found for becoming peaceful is rhythmic belly breathing in a circular breath pattern. This works by stimulating our relaxation response, which stops adrenaline and cortisol from releasing into our blood stream. The chemical basis for anxiety and fear is adrenaline, so if we stop the production of adrenaline, there is no chemistry to support feeling anxious or stressed.

To practice this breathing method effectively, set aside a time when you'll have no appointments, other activities or outside distractions. Then lie down on your back (supporting your neck and/or knees with a pillow if you need it); make sure your spine is straight. Close your eyes and become aware of your breathing. Always breathing through your nose, let your breath fill your belly on the inhale, and let the inhale curve into the exhale. On the exhale flatten the belly down all the way. Curve the exhale into the inhale. Continue doing this circular breath in a slow waltz rhythm.

On the inhale, as the belly rises, the air rushes into the lungs. But since the diaphragm is actually pulling down, it is the lower lobes of the lungs that fill with air. The lower lobes contain seven times more air (and thus oxygen) than the upper lobes. As well, the physical activity of the belly rising and falling stimulates the nerve ganglia in the lower abdomen, activating the relaxation response.

As you are doing the rhythmic belly breathing, thoughts will come and go, but don't get involved in them. Just notice them and let them pass by, like so many clouds drifting across the sky. Keep your attention on your breathing. Eventually your breathing will automatically slow and you'll slip into a deeply relaxed state. As your mind gradually empties, you may begin to notice pleasant sensations of tingling and light. You may even have a dream or symbolic vision. Let yourself go with the flow of your inner experience. [See Appendix for more detailed and more advanced instructions for this breath method: "The Breath of Life: A Path to Inner Peace."]

Once you've calmed yourself through meditation or belly-breathing, you begin to notice with detachment what goes on in your mind. You can sort out what are imaginings, fantasies, desires, thoughts and motives as opposed to the heart's promptings. You can identify urges that come from addiction, self-destructiveness, fears, false beliefs or wishful thinking. You can gain insight into whether or not they are valid, and then let them go. Self-destructive patterns of belief and fear are replaced by insight and the experience of being in inner peace. Deep peace connects us with the ground of our being, with infinity, with a felt sense of the benevolence of the universe.

Allying with the Deeper Mind for Healing and Insight

Beneath the level of the conscious mind is the pre-conscious mind – that part of our mind which we can access when we're completely relaxed. In popular literature it is often referred to as the subconscious mind. Beneath that is the unconscious mind. Together, these make up about 90% of the mind. The deeper mind is quite brilliant. But you have to give it a chance to show this brilliance, by first quieting the conscious mind. With the controlled rhythmic breath, we can accelerate how quickly we work through everything weighing on our mind. The unconscious mind starts helping with solutions to problems or with creative visions: these just appear in the mind's eye.

When we're in a deep state of peace we can access our deeper mind. We can ask questions and get answers or insight from it; and we can receive Inner Guidance, however it appears. Ask any question you like – about relationships, work, next steps, what's underneath some discomfort (physical or psychological) – and wait for an answer. It may appear in your mind's eye as a symbol, picture, or word, or you may receive a feeling or sensation or sudden insight or knowingness. If you don't understand the answer, sit with it for a while. Notice all you can about it – its color, size, shape, the various meanings you associate with it. Notice any other images, words or feelings that come along. Gather this information, gently letting the information come to mind, and by and by, the message will become clear to you. Whatever form the answer takes, trust that it has meaning in relation to your question.

The Inner Child Awaits

The foundation for psychological issues that inhibit us in adult life are usually laid in childhood. Of course, trauma can happen at any stage of life, and this needs to be addressed differently from how we address early childhood issues. Not all adults have grown out of childhood, and thus remain immature. Many adults have an inner child that continues to influence their adult behavior. From a dialogue with the inner child, you can understand what childhood patterns are still influencing your adult life and start to change them.

The inner child waits to be noticed. In your mind's eye you can directly contact your inner child and communicate with him or her. The inner child will be very direct and honest about what the trouble is and what he or she wants from you, the adult, now standing in as parent. The child will tell you straightaway what he or she fears or needs, and will reveal beliefs formed with child-logic that have carried over into adult life.

In communicating with our inner child through the mind's eye, we can give the him or her the parenting we didn't receive during our actual childhood. This work is important because our inner children are really part of us. Until they get what they need they remain dissociated, though still influencing our behavior, keeping us from full maturity, from using our full potential. Once we reparent them, they integrate into our psyche and we gain a fuller sense of ourselves.

To reparent your inner child, lie down or sit quietly, bring your awareness inside, breathe in your belly, quiet the mind, and go into peacefulness. As mentioned earlier, quieting the mind may take a little practice. It may take a few sessions of doing nothing but breathing in the belly for twenty or thirty minutes, calming down and letting distracting thoughts clear out. After the mental chatter and noise gives way to peacefulness and emptiness, stay with this deeper level for a minute or two. You can hold the space by focusing on your breath in the belly, slowly letting the belly rise on the inhale, fall on the exhale. Then mentally ask to receive an image or sense of your inner child. You can say something like, "Little (name), I am here for you. I want to talk to you. Will you come talk with me?" Then wait until you have a sense of the child's presence. It can be a felt sense, or an image appearing in your mind's eye. You may receive very clear images, depending on how much you've developed your inner visioning muscle. When this sense or image appears, ask your inner child to talk to you. Stay in your deep space; don't go into mental intellectualizing. Then, just being receptive, pay attention to what he or she says.

The child knows precisely what s/he wants or needs and will tell you. You need only be a wise parent and find the best way to provide what s/he needs, in your mind's eye. He may need loving words, understanding, attention, comfort, or even for you to go with him or her in your imagination to a place to play or to have some other experience important for his growth. For example, in your imagination, you can go with the child to the beach, the zoo, a birthday party, or whatever works to help him have the needed experience. Your inner child may want you to vanquish some scary monster, which you, as adult, can do with whatever envisioned method comes to mind. Maybe you just lock the monster in a cage and toss it into the sea. Imagination comes in handy here, and it all works, for reasons I will explain below. You can give reassurances that you, the adult or "big" (name) will be there for him or her. Close the session by saying you will be back soon to talk some more with the inner child.

Sometimes our inner children want us to do things which are inappropriate or not good for them, or they test boundaries by becoming very demanding. Don't let them take over. At such times, "sit down" with them for a little talk, and parent them the same way you would an actual child. Instead of allowing the child to indulge in inappropriate behavior, you can set limits and explain so the child understands what's good for him or her.

Inner children are more quickly satisfied than actual children because they don't live in linear time. We can, for instance, go with them on a trip to the beach in our imagination, all in about a minute by our time. But in that minute, our inner child has a complete experience. As we reparent our child, we see him or her grow up. He or she may need several experiences at various early ages which you yourself did not get in real life. These experiences enable him to complete childhood developmental stages and become fully present as an adult, integrated into your own personality. Once you bring the inner child up to the present time, the inner child is subsumed into your whole being and is integrated into your adult personality. You'll feel the energy and aliveness of the child, once cut off from your adult experience, now enlivening your adult self.

In doing the inner child work, you are tapping into and working with the unconscious mind. The unconscious doesn't "think" in the usual way; it reacts. Because it can't distinguish between reality and unreality it absorbs all the information received through the senses as true, as real.

We form memories when an experience is emotionally charged and we assign a meaning to it. As you may already know, the mind is not the brain. The brain is merely the "hardware" through which the mind, or consciousness operates. How this hardware works, or physically how memories are formed, is still somewhat of a mystery. What is known is that memories are stored physically in the brain, electro-biochemically and in neural connections in specific patterns, or networks. Recent research has associated the process with changes in the flow of electrical charges, or ions (Na, K, Mg, Ca), across the nerve membrane. Dr. Benjamin Treadwell reports that exactly how a thought process or input from our environment produces this movement is not yet fully understood. But the more intense or impressive the thought or observation, the more sustained the electrical charge. (Treadwell, 2011)

We know the brain has plasticity. We can change neural pathways in the physical brain, forming new pathways and shutting down old pathways of thought. In the 1970s, Donald Hebb, Ph.D., a Canadian neuropsychologist, presented a theory of learning and memory based on the nature of synaptic transmissions in the central nervous system. According to Hebb, when we learn new information, we change the relationship between neurons. Thought patterns fire specific neural networks in particular areas of the brain.

To the subconscious mind, picturing something and actually experiencing it are equivalent. So when we do inner child work, we actually give the inner child a new meaningful experience. The brain records these impressions by firing new neural networks, which sets up new patterns of thought. We re-wire our brain by "giving" different and new experiences to the inner child. Since inner child memories comprise the foundation for adult patterns of behavior and beliefs, changing the patterns at the early level cascades up through the patterns built upon them, up into adult life, thus changing our life.

If inner child work appeals to you but you have difficulty doing it on your own, you can get help from someone trained in clinical hypnotherapy, "Focusing" (a Gendlin technique) or somatic therapy. The next chapter discusses these types of therapy.

The Path Not Taken

After I'd undergone various kinds of therapies, and after I did the inner child work, Guidance pushed me to take another step. I had never gotten over regrets about how my life had gone, how I wished I'd been given advantages some people were given, advantages I couldn't help but envy…

I was guided to run a mind's eye "movie" of my inner child, rescripting the movie to see how it would go had things been different for me. I envisioned the inner child going through life receiving all the acknowledgement and support I had craved. I watched her grow into adulthood up to my current age in 1996, but having taken another path.

Here's how my life had actually gone: I was disaffected with the so-called American Dream at a very early age, having seen what happened to parents of the Fifties who conformed to the nine-to-five working dad and stay-at-home mom program. In my own family, there were all the typical Fifties family dysfunctions – too much alcohol and cigarettes included. Dad was emotionally unavailable;

Mom was bored once the nest was empty, but had neither the courage nor the support to make a new life for herself. She died when I was sixteen. The stepmother who replaced her was selfish and cruel to me and my siblings and emotionally castrating toward my father. We three siblings acted out all the unexpressed unhappiness of the two parents, taking it out on each other.

Ultimately, family cohesion came with a big price: no one was permitted to talk about anything painful or difficult. Keeping up appearances was all important to Mom and Dad. I was disturbed by the hypocrisy and pretense of everything being fine when it really wasn't. On some subliminal level, I felt all the hidden pain of my family members. Being told regularly, "If you can't say something nice, don't say anything at all," and being told frequently I was "too sensitive," I eventually stopped trying to make myself seen or heard. To get along in the family, I realized I'd best keep my mouth shut, and make my own way in life if I wanted to preserve my individuality.

One very great blessing though, was that we lived in an upper middle class safe neighborhood, within walking distance of good schools. The economy was robust, enjoying the spoils of World War II and the competitive edge that winning the war had given to the United States. Materially, the quality of life was good, but psychologically, it was, to me, empty, falsified and repressive. "Propriety" was so important that we were not permitted even to read *Mad Magazine*, an American humor comic book (launched as a magazine years later). It satirized the entire cultural landscape of the 1950s, and was the only voice of dissent I had access to in the conservative suburbs of Southern California where we lived. To me it was a breath of fresh air! Our neighborhood gang was determined to have these comics, so we decided to have a "scavenger hunt," which surely all our parents would approve of. We made up the list of items we'd ask the neighbors to give to us, like clothespins and other silly items, if they had them to give. Far down on the list we included *Mad Magazine*. Our scavenge was successful, and we took our considerable stack of *Mad Magazine*'s to the cave one our the neighborhood gang members had dug under his back yard. There we read the magazines by flashlight, undetected by our very proper parents.

By age fifteen, I began holding summer jobs. I put myself through college with part-time work, with some student loan assistance, which I later paid back. I went to good schools and had excellent teachers, a great blessing for which I will be eternally grateful. But a college degree in political science offered little in the way of career path. Available jobs were with the government, and this was during the era of the Vietnam War. There was no way I was going to work for a government that was engaged in what I believe was an illegal and immoral war. Instead, following graduation from Stanford, I became an investigative journalist, then a magazine editor, then returned to school for a graduate degree in Clinical Psychology.

So, in later years, when I did the "path not taken" work, I scripted my movie to see how I would have fared had I had all the support and understanding I wanted from my parents, the financial support I would have liked so I could have concentrated more on my studies without having to work part-time, and maybe I could have gone on to more advanced education. The path not taken would have been the conventional one of having the family, PhD, mainstream career, and probably more cultural pursuits along the way, like more training as a musician.

After I ran that "movie," and compared it with my actual life, I could see that my actual life path of many zigs and zags, much improvisation, and learning many survival skills, brought me right to where I would have ended up via the path not taken, but my zigs and zags had given me much richer experience. So really it was a better path to have taken. I'd done it right all along. Doing this exercise enabled me to dispel regrets I'd had about the path I'd actually taken, and I've had no regrets since.

Fear is the Obstacle to Peacefulness

To have lasting peace of mind, we need to remove obstacles to peace – and the biggest is fear. It comes in all kinds of disguises. But fear usually boils down to one fear only – the fear of death. If we face that, other fears seem trivial in comparison. To overcome the fear of death is one of the most empowering experiences we can have. We could go happily to our graves if we'd done everything we wanted to do in life, had a clear conscience, and had spent ourselves so thoroughly we were happy for a rest. This is not to suggest we court death or be reckless or careless, of course. But we can face our own death in imagination, find out pretty clearly what our attitude toward it is, and come to terms with it. Then we'll be well on the way to living without fear.

To do this, set aside a half hour, lie down comfortably on your back, and direct your attention inward. Calm yourself by breathing in the belly until your mind clears. Then focus on your mind's eye. Picture yourself at the edge of your grave. Notice what else goes through your mind – feelings, thoughts, images or sensations. Next, look back at your life. Start from your early years and continue on through the entire life you imagine you will have lived. Review the significant events, relationships and accomplishments, and then ask yourself if you're satisfied with how you lived. Did anything remain undone that was important? Was there anything you wished you hadn't done or need to make amends for? This exercise brings vividly to mind all the things we truly want to be and do before our life is over. Failure to fulfill our earthly lives is all we need regret.

Meditative peaceful states achieved through belly breathing and clearing the mind's eye can be used for any internal work anytime we want to solve a problem in our emotional or spiritual life, tap into our creativity, or gain insight. The mind's eye is where we access the intelligence provided by the body-mind. Our body-mind makes meaning from millions of bits of information coming through our nervous system, from our environment, our intuition, and from the whole of our experience, stored as memory.

> *"The imagination is probably a person's least utilized health resource. It can be used to remember and recreate the past, develop insight into the present, influence physical health, enhance creativity and inspiration, and anticipate possible futures."*
>
> ~ Dr. Martin Rossman, co-founder of the
> Academy for Guided Imagery

Playing it Out in the Mind's Eye

When asked what they wish for, most people say they want to be rich. Yet what would they do with their money? Take fancy vacations, live in splendor, throw lavish parties, eat at Four Star restaurants, wear silk, tell servants what to do, have sexy lovers every night? If we imagine we really want these experiences, we owe it to ourselves to find a way to have them, *as long as* they do not come at someone else's expense. But it may suffice merely to have the experience, wealth, or whatever you desire fulfilled in your imagination. You can play it out in the mind's eye, visualizing the whole experience, with feelings and sensory details, in your own virtual reality. Then, based on that experience, you can decide whether to pursue it or not. This is a risk-free, cost-free way of exploring whether the imagined pleasures would truly satisfy or fulfill your heart's desire.

Before committing to a path you're not sure about, you can further explore how it would fit for you by interviewing people in your ideal profession or by doing an internship. Find out what it really takes. If you think you want to be a doctor, for instance, you should actively seek answers to questions like, "What would it be like if I were a doctor?" "Would I enjoy doing what a doctor does?" "Would I enjoy learning what a doctor has to learn?" "Would I gain satisfaction from taking care of people's medical needs?" Or say you imagine you'd love to be a concert pianist, but you find no time to play the piano. More likely you're in love with the idea of being a pianist but aren't committed to practicing.

Many people work hard for things they believe they want and then find they don't want them after all. Or they imagine they want a certain career but don't do anything to make it happen. Many people will embark on a career path that isn't so much what they want as what someone else told them they should want. If they continue, they sacrifice the opportunity to find fulfillment. To find what we really want, to fulfill our potential and true calling, we need to take our desires seriously.

If we can't imagine what gives us satisfaction, we haven't properly identified our deepest desires. Everything we want or care about reveals something about us. It's not negative, but positive selfishness to pay attention to what we want. Looking after ourselves is imperative if we want to live fully. Psychological and spiritual growth happen in the process of discovering who we are, our purpose, and in identifying our special gifts and potential.

When we live according to our heart's desire, our process is as compelling as the result. We enjoy getting there as much as being there. According to spiritual principles, our life work is to learn and to serve, but if we don't *enjoy,* we don't learn and the quality of what we offer to others may be compromised. If we don't enjoy our work and aren't learning anything, we're in the wrong place. No occupation is too arduous if it fulfills our sense of meaning and teaches us what we want to learn.

During meditation, your mind's eye offers clues and insight into what you need in any given moment, even on the most basic level. If, for instance, you have a nutritional need, your mind's eye may present an image of a particular food or supplement we need, and how much we should take.* It can be quite specific. For example, one afternoon in the midst of a mid-afternoon energy slump I asked what I needed. In my mind's eye I received an image of seven sunflower seeds in the palm of my hand! Sunflower seeds contain fluorine, which gives a boost to wake you up.

If you face relationship issues, your mind's eye can show you the problem and guide you in how to take care of yourself. It can show you what's making you afraid or angry, or what you need that you're not getting. Your mind's eye can give you a picture of what's amiss. You might see an image of two people (stick figures will do). Perhaps one is bigger and seems to be overpowering, while the other is bent low. Or perhaps the image of a bar or wall appears between the two people, symbolizing a communication barrier. Perhaps there's a red light between the two figures, symbolizing anger or hidden resentment that needs to be aired.

[*author's note: The topic of proper nutrition and supplementation is beyond the scope of this book. There is much literature available to the reader seriously interested in restoring physical health. It will be common sense to anyone who acquaints himself with the dangers of consuming food that is pesticide-laden, has chemical additives, GMO food ingredients, and other food toxins, to avoid these foods. Instead, eat organic food whenever possible and avoid processed foods. What I learned from my four years of intensive physical healing using nutrition, herbs and various supplements, is that healing the body proceeds in a step-by-step order. There is a precise order in which each depleted organ must be healed, a precise order in which nutritional deficiencies must be remediated. Every individual is unique, so one size does not fit all. Diagnoses by traditional medical practitioners are limited to the tools and training available to them, which themselves are rather limited. Therefore, there are many

benefits to be had from combining traditional medical knowledge with natural medicine and perhaps input from a skilled medical intuitive.]

Living in the Present

When we've worked through our psychological issues, we can get in touch with our purpose, with what we really think, feel and want. And the path we are meant to travel is revealed, one step at a time.

No one can predict the future. We can guess at probable outcomes, but we can't know what lies ahead, beyond what is apparent through ordinary analysis. Since all individuals have free will, the human population is like one big organism with many mov-ing parts and processes! But if we become fully aware in the present, we'll know how to proceed to the next step. As in a hologram, each part contains the whole. The present moment contains the potential for all that might unfold before us.

Fear and anxiety constrict our awareness, narrowing our focus, cutting off the flow of information. We lose sight of the big picture and our perspective becomes distorted. Stress hormones are released and hormone balance is affected. Emotionality clouds our thinking and perceiving. Being peaceful in the present moment is the only way to stay in touch with all the information available to us through our five senses as well as through our intuition and Inner Guidance.

CHAPTER 4.

DEEP HEALING

For people who have had severely traumatic experiences, consulting a psychotherapist can be especially helpful for your healing. A skilled therapist can facilitate your going into a deep quiet state and help you access a past experience through internal imagery. The therapist provides the emotional safety which is essential to being able to re-experience trauma in order to heal it. You can re-visit the traumatic event from a safe shore, from a distance, as if you were watching a movie, rather than actually re-living the experience. This way, you don't get retraumatized. Through this work, you can understand the meaning you assigned to the childhood experience, correct the child's interpretation if that interpretation was erroneous, and the therapist or our adult self can give the healing/corrective experience to the inner child.

A negative experience during childhood may have been traumatic or painful. But the part we carry into adulthood is only memory, stored in electro-chemical form, in networks of neurons, and can therefore be changed. If, for example, we remember the trauma of a parent not helping us when we needed it, we can go into our psychic memory bank, call up the memory, give the needed help via our mind's eye, and resolve the trauma. This is similar in process to changing data in a computer file. This only works if we remember what actually happened, what we felt about it and the belief we formed as a result. We must see enough of the past scenario in our mind's eye, feel the feelings connected with it, and understand the meaning we took from the experience before we can change it. Otherwise, we achieve nothing more than the temporary brainwashing achieved by most "positive affirmation" methods. To complete the healing experience, we must gain a felt sense of power and mastery over the specific form of victimization, guilt or anxiety we experienced earlier.

Insight through talk therapy and insight from accessing the physical memory are not mutually exclusive methods. In my experience they are complementary. Trauma contains both a mental and a physical component. It isn't a case of either-or.

Focusing Technique

Dr. Eugene Gendlin, philosopher and psychotherapist, said, "There's no therapy that can't be made better by referencing the body." Gendlin coined the term "the felt sense" in his 1978 book, *Focusing.* In "focusing" work, one goes into a deep quiet space, focuses awareness inside the body, and then pays attention to any felt sense one notices. This could be tension, tingling, discomfort or dis-ease in the body. Next, one amplifies one's sense of it by noticing everything about the sensation – where it is, its shape, color, feeling, any associated image that arises… simply watching and noticing. The felt sense bridges to the associated emotion, and then to the past experience, however it is represented. The latter may show up as a clear memory or simply as a symbolic image in which is contained the entire complex at the root of our discomfort or pathogenic belief. One can decode it as one might interpret a dream. The "encoded" experience contains the meaning; once we understand the meaning we are able to resolve and integrate the experience. The focusing method is simple but powerful, and is a good place to start for those who are just beginning their inner work. (Gendlin, 1981)

Clinical Hypnosis and Somatic Therapy

Another powerful "body oriented" therapeutic approach was developed by Dr. Peter Levine. Dr. Levine pioneered work in the field of clinical hypnosis. I took a workshop with him in the 1990's. At that time he taught that during the hypnotherapeutic session it was important for the patient to understand all the aspects of a "retrieved" early experience before it could be fully resolved or healed. One had to become conscious of the sensation, the image, the behavior, the affect (emotion), and the meaning the individual assigned to the experience. Dr. Levine used the acronym SIBAM for the five necessary elements.

In my experience of the method, in a deep hypnotic state of recalling an early traumatic experience, I re-experienced a time when I was five years old. The image memory was of me standing in front of the refrigerator at home, with the refrigerator door open.

The refrigerator appeared enormous to me. Standing next to me was an equally enormous Mom, glaring at me and commanding me to fix my lunch. I had no idea how to fix lunch. I was terrified. In real time, in the workshop, I started to go into hyperventilation, as the fear expressed itself. Dr. Levine put his hand on my stomach, gently getting me to focus on the belly breathing, and I calmed down. At the same time, to my great surprise, the taste and smell of pesticide came out on my breath. When I was a child, every Spring Dad sprayed Malathion, a very nasty pesticide, to kill aphids on rose bushes in our back yard. I had inhaled these fumes for several years. And now they came out! So two things were accomplished during this hypnotic session; the fear of angry Mom was released, as well as the pesticide that had accumulated in my body.

Since then, Dr. Levine has further developed his work. His current approach is called "Somatic Experiencing" (SE). SE is based upon the study of normal instinctive behaviors. Rather than talking things through, it focuses on where in the body the trauma is stored.

In Levine's work, it is not the dredging up and reliving of painful memories head-on that heals. He cautions that plunging directly into a full-on re-living can be re-traumatizing. SE focuses on where in the body we are "frozen" – a frightening or life-threatening experience may have caused us to freeze physiologically in the face of overwhelming threat (think of a deer in the headlights). This frozen energy must be released by converting it into an "active successful escape."

According to Dr. Levine,

> "Somatic Experiencing" alters these fixated immobility reactions – human panic and post-traumatic reactions – by neutralizing fear-potentiated freezing. It accomplishes this by uncoupling an individual's immobility response from internally generated fear. This allows the immobility (post-traumatic) reactions to complete as they do normally with animals in the wild.
>
> …When we are overwhelmed by threat, our bodies and nervous systems activate life-preserving survival responses. If we are unable to complete these innate "action plans," then we cannot discharge the vast amount of energy mobilized to do so. When this occurs, we retain in our bodies and minds undischarged residual energy, which, in turn, manifests itself as the symptoms of trauma. (Levine 1996)

Once we access the deeper mind, we have to unfreeze and then effectively defend ourselves or successfully escape from danger. The safety provided by the presence of the therapist allows us to re-visit the scene of the trauma, while not getting overwhelmed by it. Finally, what is needed, according to Levine, is to "arouse our deep physiological resources and consciously utilize them, rather than remaining ignorant of our power to change the course of our instinctual responses in a proactive rather than reactive way." (Levine, 1996, 2010) If the therapist provides the proper container, or safe space, for the therapy client, the client's own innate healing process goes forward.

Intellect finds a way to implement our plan. But we can't understand anything merely through intellect. It can only make calculations and patterns using logic, memory and ideas abstracted from reality. Intellect doesn't tell us what to do – it helps us do what the greater intelligence of our body-mind has already decided.

Growing into full selfhood, full maturity, takes slow, careful work. If we run along the path of spiritual evolution, toward enlightenment, we miss important details. We'll go too fast or focus too much on the goal. What's directly at our feet may be what's important. But above all, what is most important is to remain peaceful, no matter what. And then the path unfolds easily before us.

CHAPTER 5.

LIVING BY INNER GUIDANCE

Inner Guidance is available to those who achieve inner peace. Unfortunately, attaining a state of peace is difficult for many people, as daily life becomes more stressful. Economic survival challenges nearly everyone but the elite. Nonetheless, if one cultivates peacefulness and learns to receive Inner Guidance, the best ways to navigate through the shoals will become apparent.

Back before the U.S. was in such dire economic straits, I suffered a major financial crisis of my own. This was after I'd stopped being a psychotherapist and lived on savings while attempting to fashion a new career. The latter took longer than I anticipated, and I remained jobless until I was nearly flat broke.

I sent out dozens of resumes for work as a writer/editor, to no avail. Most of the jobs listed in the classified ads looked awful. I became quite depressed. Accepting a low-level office job just wouldn't do. I'd never be able to fake being happy at such jobs, and any employer would think me over-qualified. In my early working days I'd gotten fired from a few secretarial jobs when my then-husband was going to grad school. My bosses did not appreciate my lack of enthusiasm. One boss fired me for having a "cavalier" attitude, which meant not being obsequiously ingratiating to him and his friends.

As my joblessness continued I contacted the woman who had healed me physically and given me other guidance, hoping she might now have some helpful advice. She said I should get mad at God for not helping me find something I could take to the bank and *cash.* She advised me to tell Him how much money I needed and that I was angry at being lead along. It sounded plausible.

"I can do that?" I asked.

"Yes."

"Oh, thank you so much."

Addressing the Almighty, I said, "Okay, if I get to say how much money I want, make that $200,000 per year, starting immediately!" Anger rose inside me. "Am I angry enough yet?" I asked my inner self. "No," came the answer. I stormed some more. Soon the acid from anger was eating at my stomach. At that moment I remembered I didn't have any problem being angry. I had been angry with God until I was forty. I knew how to get angry better than most anyone. Instead of being angry and demanding, what I needed was to learn to trust the universe and the connectedness of everything. I needed to trust that the connected web of life would be responsive to my needs.

The proverbial carrot was dangled from a stick. A small consulting job was offered me. Oh, joy! I had been saved. "Yes, we love you", the employer said. "And we'll pay you. A lot. Soon." "Soon" was rescheduled for the indefinite future, and the job never materialized. I reminded myself to stay peaceful. I re-read the words I'd written in the original manuscript of this book:

> *Peacefulness allows our intuition to speak to us. Intuition is another word for inner knowing, for that which is not intellect or emotion. It draws from all the information embedded in our consciousness.*
>
> *Intuition comes as messages that have particular meaning at a particular moment, in response to a question we've asked. But we must ask a question. This sets in motion the forces which bring us the answer.*

I knew this was true. I had experienced it dozens of times. I had encountered the stranger-with-the-answer to a question within thirty minutes of my posing the question. I had seen books "glow" on library shelves that contained exactly what I needed to know at the time. I had received the entire book outline in my mind's eye for a book I wanted to write.

After months of penury, I moved from Marin County, where there was no work, to San Francisco. I began applying for entry level positions at various large companies. Though quite humbling, it gave me the chance to learn computer skills which I would need ongoing. Then Guidance told me to explore what I really wanted to do to make a living. This was at the start of the Internet boom, and I realized I wanted to be part of this industry. Within a short time, I secured a high paying job as managing editor at a start-up company. Within a few months, that company went bankrupt. Immediately I was offered a job at another tech start-up. There, I learned a lot and was paid quite well, but management started implementing irrational dumb policies. As a result, I couldn't tolerate the job for long and I quit. Right away I secured a position as Executive Editor at another tech company. This lasted a few months. But then the owners of the company artificially inflated the price of their stock, using creative accounting, spent all the venture capital, then sold their shares at a great profit and laid off all the employees. I suspected their whole scheme had been planned many months before they finally took the money and ran.

Then came the dot-com crash (which I had foreseen, given how venture capitalists were throwing money at businesses they didn't understand and which were often pretty stupid businesses). Again, I lived on savings and continued applying for jobs. The economy of the San Francisco Bay Area was dismal. Shortly thereafter, there were the World Trade Center attacks of September 11, 2001, and things spiraled downward. San Francisco is heavily dependent on tourism, and people weren't "touring" – no one wanted to fly in an airplane. My savings dwindled to close to nothing, and despite my best efforts, there were no jobs to be had for people with my skills. (I really didn't want to go back to being a psychotherapist.)

To allay my great fear of being broke again, I spent a lot of time in meditation. One of the most effective techniques was to visualize burning up my fear in a bonfire. The bonfire represented God. This transmutes emotion by turning it over to a Higher Power. It worked, to a point. But fear still came up: fear of being homeless (that was the worst); fear I'd have no one in my corner. To these were added old childhood fears – fear of being deceived, abandoned, exploited, judged and found lacking, and so forth.

I told myself not to be disappointed. I was still a work in progress. I shouldn't get attached to outcomes. "Be omni-visioning," I told myself. "See all possibilities. Be open to opportunity." Sage advice, to be sure, but this meant being happy with no empirical evidence to justify it. I was supposed to let positive expectation work on the unseen plane to bring me to situations and opportunities that could help. I reminded myself not to dismiss chance encounters or opportunities. I needed to be open to inspiration, to learning something new, to some new door opening. This was real calisthenics in right-thinking, as the Buddhists say.

In addition to regular meditation, I did a lot of belly breathing, in a fast rhythm, throughout the day, in order to neutralize the fear adrenaline by super-oxygenating. This proved to be extremely effective. Once the adrenaline was neutralized by the extra oxygen, I no longer felt afraid but felt calm again and able to receive clear Inner Guidance. In hindsight, I see that this ordeal was an essential part of my journey, for it taught me a good deal of fearlessness. I do, at this stage of my life, trust that I am well looked after by the Almighty, and since that period of "trials by fire," my trust has been well rewarded.

What happened, finally, was that Inner Guidance led me step-by-step in the process of re-building my life. First I was instructed leave the San Francisco Bay Area, which was still economically depressed. I was guided to pack only the belongings that would fit in my car – fortunately, I was driving a sedan at the time – and to go to the Ojai Foundation in Southern California. I'd imagined I'd be welcomed there as a teacher, but when I arrived, they informed me they already had enough teachers and programs. They said I could do the "Path of

Service," which meant working on the property in exchange for being able to live in a tent on the land and have daily breakfast provided. Guidance assured me this was indeed the offer for now, so I stayed for six weeks, doing gardening and kitchen detail, and sweeping mouse droppings out of the yurts occupied by paying guests.

It was actually good for me to be doing these mundane tasks. My physical fitness improved, it got me out of my head, and made me let go of a whole lot of ego! I also had to think about what I really wanted to do for work. (Again, I was prompted by Inner Guidance to get clear about this.) I concluded that my ideal job would be helping independent authors publish their books. This seemed like the next logical step after the psychotherapy career – from helping individuals work through their neuroses and psychoses, to helping authors bring forth their own body of knowledge useful for others. I'd also given more thought to the book I wanted to write next, which would be a book to bridge the gap between mysticism and science. I thought it would have to be physics that would be the bridge.

One morning I was having breakfast by myself in the kitchen cabin up near the ridge at the top of the Foundation property. Ojai Foundation property is shaped like a dragon, head at the bottom of the hill, spine and tail winding up the hill, ending at the top of a ridge. As I was sitting eating, I heard some odd loud grunting sounds just outside the cabin, coming from the trail that ran up the length of the property. Wondering if the property had been invaded by an intruder – human or animal – I stepped outside the kitchen to look. There was a man walking down the trail, with a shirt wrapped turban-style around his head, presumably to protect his scalp from the intense October sunlight. As I soon learned, he was doing Qi Gong, and the sounds were part of it. The fellow appeared civilized enough, so I hailed him and invited him to join me for breakfast.

It turned out that he and his son were spending the weekend at the Foundation. He was, he told me, a quantum physicist and wanted to write a book on "quantum spirit," about using quantum physics to explain the dimension of spirit. I told him I had wanted for some time to write a book on the physics of metaphysics but did not know enough physics. I also told him I was an editor and book designer and could produce his book for him. What are the odds of a meeting like that? This project sounded ideal to us both, and so we struck a deal.

I relocated to Pasadena, where he lived. He invited me to stay in his in-law unit, in partial exchange for my work. We started with his manuscript on healing and quantum biophysics. In the process of editing and producing his book I learned a fair amount of quantum physics, exactly what I'd wanted. (We never did get to the "Quantum Spirit" book.)

This project complete, it was time for my next move. Inner Guidance told me, "You're moving to Santa Monica. Start looking at online rental listings." While I was doing so, Guidance pointed out two rentals to visit. The first was ghastly – cramped, with constant traffic noise from the street outside the window. I hoped this experience was merely to provide a basis for comparison. That turned out to be the case. While driving to the next appointment in Santa Monica, I kept hearing, "Close the deal." When I arrived at the designated address, another person was there interviewing for the rental. While showing us both the apartment, the leaseholder kept pointing out things that needed fixing. I kept saying, "Oh, that's okay." Suffice it to say, I got the place. It turned out to be the needle-in-a-haystack kind of find. It suited my limited budget (not an easy thing in Westside Los Angeles!) It was situated in a walkable neighborhood four blocks from the ocean. The apartment was bathed by fresh ocean air, and had west-facing rooms which were sunny and bright. It was relatively quiet, which is quite important to me. And best of all, the leaseholder was almost never there initially, and a bit later, was *never* there, so it became virtually my place…at a price I could afford.

When it came time for me to get another car, to replace the one I'd been driving that was too old to be worth repairing, I was guided to the perfect car, on Ebay, yet! It was a used Prius, at half the price other sellers were asking. Virtually the same day as I made the decision to purchase that car, the bank offered me a loan to cover the amount, at zero interest for a year. The car has been perfect for me. No buyer's remorse!

Even building my publishing business anew after arriving in Santa Monica has been fairly effortless. One introduction led to other introductions, each of which was important. Author clients have come to me as if by some higher orchestration, each one teaching me as much as I teach them. And what I've learned from each of these publishing projects is precisely what I wanted to learn and seems to follow a progression taylored to my own growth (as well as theirs).

Ongoing, I continue to be impressed by how much easier my life has been in following Inner Guidance. I'm continually struck by how much more efficiently I can get tasks and projects done, because Guidance saves me going through hit-and-misses, the ordinary trial-and-error process. The time this frees allows me to move quickly and enjoyably along my path. Life has become a process of just staying the course, one day at a time, and seeing what unfolds before me.

Distinguishing Imagination from Divine Guidance

The efficacy of the guidance we receive depends on how well we listen. It isn't always easy to quiet the mind. Our imagination is forever inventing stories and scenarios. The ego tries to run the show. Emotions and desires distort our thoughts.

True Inner Guidance is the voice of God within. God helps in the tiniest details, in the grand scheme of our lives and everything in between. Details are never a problem, nor is the size or scope of an effort or plan. There are myriad paths to an ongoing conversation or partnership with God, but they all converge at the same sacred place – one of inner silence and receptivity.

Be patient. Sit and just watch your thoughts and impressions pass like scudding clouds, without getting involved in them. Eventually emotions and mental chatter fade away and your mind becomes still. That is the time to pose your question or ask for help. Before asking your question, *it is important to state mentally that all information must come only from the highest source.*

The Creator will answer. Sometimes the answer comes as an insight or realization, sometimes an intuitive knowing, sometimes as an image, sometimes as words or thoughts in the mind's eye which are distinct from our own. Sometimes the answers come as opportunities or events, such as people with answers to our dilemmas or questions, books on a shelf drawing our attention, friends bringing the very item or assistance we need. Perhaps a job opportunity will arise that provides access to exactly what we need to experience or learn.

How can we know if the messages we receive are from God, as opposed to our imagination or wishful thinking? If your mind is sufficiently still you can tell the difference. If verbal, the message(s) you receive will have a different quality or tone. The message may be a style of speaking that is not your own, or may contain information entirely new to you. The verbal messages I receive are like "words of air," having a quality distinctly different from my own thoughts. It requires a still mind to make such distinctions.

If you are not sure whether the information is truly coming from the highest Source, or God, or if it's just your imagination, then return to empty mind and ask again. If you are still not sure, repeat the process. If you receive the same answer three times, consider it trustworthy.

Who Really Talks to God?

Unfortunately, the phenomenon of "talking with God" has, on occasion, gotten a bad name. In my experience some people who proclaim publicly that they receive messages from God have not done sufficient inner work to clarify their psyche and resolve their emotional issues. Their pronouncements, projections, and prophesies are usually incoherent, self-serving and self-contradictory. If you examine the personal history of these unclarified people, you can discover what motivates them to claim God as their authority. They may be running from something in themselves and hiding behind what they believe to be God's authority. Religious zeal, for another thing, is a dead give-away that these individuals are being driven by something irrational. The unreflective reactivity expressed by extremist groups is quite destructive. In these groups you see the naked id erupting without the rationalizing influence of the mature personality, the mature healthy ego structure. People who are crazy are not hearing God…

Is There a Higher Intelligence?

This raises one obvious question: Is there is a Higher Intelligence that can give direction, or is it merely the "God in all things" working through nature, according to the laws of physics and biology? I posit that it is all of this. According to information I have received from Source, or God, God is a Directing Intelligence who oversees the entire firmament and directs the course of evolution. But God does not determine our existence. According to what I've received, He/She does consider a local plan or two here and there. He/She acts as would a conductor with an orchestra. There is a bigger plan, a master plan for our continued evolution. The scope and means of this are beyond our comprehension, however, except through hindsight and long-term observation. The Creator's awareness, too, is in constant flux, constantly changing, mixing, shifting gears.

We, the players in the orchestra, are motivated to follow the conductor, insofar as that seems to benefit the whole. So all of us individual entities with our distinct personalities always have a choice about tuning in with the conductor or not.

Every creature is full of God
And is a book about God.
Every creature is a word of God.

All creatures flow outward,
but nonetheless remain within God.
Everything that is in God, is God.
God is a being beyond Being
and a Nothingness beyond Being.
God's being is my being
And God's primordial being
Is my primordial being.

Because this Word is a hidden Word.
It comes in the darkness of the night.
To enter this darkness put away
All voices and sounds
All images and likenesses
In stillness and peace
In this unknowing knowledge
God speaks in the soul.

~ Meister Eckhart, translated by Mathew Fox

CHAPTER 6.

MORE ADVANCED MEDITATION

I've continued my meditation and receive Inner Guidance daily. In following the Guidance, I have all my needs provided for and am able to do the work I love. As well, my meditations have deepened and provided more benefits. Given this, here follows material on more advanced meditation and the rewards one may experience from practicing.

But first the context. In 2003, I was receiving daily information from Inner Guidance, Source, as well as telepathic communication from other sentient beings. One day I received a pretty extensive telepathic communication from a man I'd never met in person – and never did meet – who said he lived in Marin County, just north of San Francisco. At the time, I was researching and writing about meditation and intuition. Besides validating the reality and value of telepathy, the information about meditation was so incisive and instructive I am including it in this book, whole cloth.

He introduced himself to me telepathically as Dr. Stan Ellsberg. He said his message was meant to be instructive for my clients and patients.

Though I was no longer a practicing psychotherapist, I was still offering counseling to a few people, using the messages, images and insights from Inner Guidance, Source, in conjunction with my own expertise as a psychologist. You might say I was (and still am) practicing as a spiritual intuitive. Dr. Ellsberg told me the following:

How erroneous thinking may be most effectively cleared, without years of talk therapy

1. Begin by sitting in Vipassana – using the breath is good. *[author's note: Vipassana is a meditation technique wherein one sits and merely notices thoughts, without getting caught up in them, just observing them and watching them go by, like clouds moving across the sky.]*

2. Notice how in deepening one gets beneath all concept of the relative.

3. Then one forms an attachment to the All That Is. That is, one becomes unified in revisiting the safety of the One Mind. It is connected to the Divine, and each time a person revisits it he or she is more aligned with the Divine.

4. Fear is equivalent to separation from the Divine. Insofar as one has conceived of the self as alone, uncared for, unprotected by the universe/God/Goddess/All That Is, one is stressed with low level anxiety, or minimal fear, up to and including abject terror. If a person seeks to build walls around him/herself, and has possessions and security systems and investments as 'security,' he

is unable to recognize how he is playing fear's game. If, on the other hand, the person simply 'experiences' the fear, the fear gives way to, again, a momentary peace, until the next bit of fear arises. And so it goes.Once fear is overcome for awhile, the person is free to enjoy his life, until he is again triggered.

5. Fear is the enemy, not criminals or gunslingers, though living in a seedy part of town might convince one otherwise. Say, though, a gang was ravaging the neighborhood. Quaking in fear is playing the fear game. Gathering your inner fortitude and doing something about the gang activity is stepping out of fear and into an act of unification with Divinity. That is, if one approaches the task from the right motivation, in the interest of peace.

6. If we have a set belief in eternal damnation, then fear is given a free ticket to sit in the balcony of our minds, ever present to judge us as being bad or failing to please the great judge in the sky. If, on the other hand, we imagine ourself essentially beneficent, and we all have that part in us, then we have a way to sit in our chair in a pleasant atmosphere, if you will.

Ellsberg continued,

Most people are in fear some or all of the time. Very few are fearless all the time – maybe 1% of the human populace. It is a known fact that fear creates stress, creates disease. All dis-ease, with the exception of chemical and environmental poisoning, results as an expression of fear, qua anxiety, qua stress – whatever you want to call it. Genetic deficiencies are not always disease-producing. Some can result in ultimate degradation of a part or several parts of the human body, but in the case of said, there has been a stimulant to start the degenerative process. If one has a genetic defect from birth, it can be stabilized with appropriate life support systems and be unclassifiable as a disease proper.

The wonderful way that meditation works includes rearranging associative neuronal pathways. If the meditator persists in regular meditation, eventually the neuronal pathways are routed more predominantly towards the portion of the brain (left cerebral cortex) associated with pleasing emotional states, and away from the part of the brain (amygdala) associated with unpleasant emotional states. A regular practice of meditation, then, can give us a secure seat, as it were, in pleasant emotional states.

Love issues forth when we are in pleasant emotional states. And if the love is directed toward resolving a particular problem, the way to fix the problem is seen more readily.

Love and peacefulness have very many manifestations. Compassion is a state of expressing love toward another being. Love is a com-passion – empathy, in other words. If a person is calm and centered or peaceful, he is able to be accurately empathic.

We don't accept the testimony of another to confirm or deny our intuitional insight. Embedded in intuition is all we know about a given situation.

When we are absolutely quiet and still we may access the understanding underlying all manifest form, or 'conventional reality.' It is a fact that underlying a convention is a common understanding, which gave rise to the convention in the first place. But what is here the obvious problem is we had little or nothing ourselves to do with stating the understanding. Ergo, convention is not a true expression of ourselves. [end of Ellsberg message]

The Six Levels of Peacefulness

We can learn much about spiritual progression, meditation, and enlightenment from the Buddhist tradition. D. T. Suzuki (1870 –1966) has been considered by many to be the greatest authority on Zen Buddhism and probably the greatest modern authority on Buddhist philosophy. While he writes about the various kinds of Buddhism, much of his work focuses on Mahayana Buddhism. In this tradition, transcendental knowledge constitutes enlightenment.

As Suzuki wrote in 1953, "[Mahayana Buddhism] is an intuition into the ultimate truth of things, by gaining which one is released from the bondage of existence and becomes master of one's self." (Suzuki 1953)

Serious students of meditation value Suzuki's description of the levels of peacefulness realized during meditation, because it provides a measure of one's progress as a meditator. Suzuki's levels of peacefulness are realized through meditative self-inquiry. I have greatly simplified these levels into 6:

1. The level of idle thought is calmed. [author: no more "monkey chatter."]

2. Next follows "what if" imaginings, such as "How can I survive if…," etc. Fear is encountered here. A level of understanding, or intellectual lucidity ensues: We gain insight into the underlying meaning of things, beneath surface appearances.

3. We move then into concentration: our mind empties for a while. Our energies focus into silent coherence.

4. Disciplining oneself in tranquilization: Having achieved a momentary concentration of energies, we reach a level of tranquility. This is disturbed again and again by thoughts that need to be observed and allowed to pass.

5. Tranquility: We eventually gain an unruffled state of peacefulness. Nothing, neither external nor internal in origin, disturbs our peacefulness.

6. This is not yet all. As Suzuki wrote, "The Yogin must be philosophically trained with all his experiences and intuitions to have a clear, logical, penetrating understanding of the Essence. When this is properly directed, he will have no more confused ideas introduced by misguided philosophers. "

Once mastering the ability to quiet and clear your mind and tuning in to your intuition, you are well on your way to receiving clear Inner Guidance from Source, or God. Perhaps you have already had experiences of being guided. Direct communication with God is everyone's birthright. Anyone can learn to do it. It's not hard, however it does require discipline. I wasn't always able to receive inner guidance. I had to learn how, and if I could learn it, then, I firmly believe, anyone can learn it.

Making Peacefulness a Priority

We must learn to remain peaceful no matter what, even in the midst of chaos or mishap. Peacefulness allows us to see our way through life's challenges and difficulties. When peaceful, the insights we receive are clearer than when we're distressed. An insight received under duress is, at best, partial or distorted. Thoughts that come or actions that are taken in the heat of emotion usually are suspect. Not to say we should live without emotion, for it provides energy for motion. However, we should not plan our lives from a base of emotion.

While being peaceful, we also must remain alert. A cat may appear peaceful and relaxed while lying in the sun, but is ever alert and can respond in an instant. So it is with us. When relaxed but not sleepy, we can sense danger before it threatens. We can act quickly if the need arises. We can dodge obstructions with agility or avoid negative situations by distancing ourselves from them.

The heart functions as one of our greatest helpmates. While the heart is a symbol of romantic love, it also is a sensitive register of positive or negative influences, even on the most subtle levels. It offers information that assists us in making wise choices. We know in our hearts if something is not right. Our heart warns us when an individual maybe negative or harmful. In that instance, it closes and defends itself. In a negative situation, our energy and optimism wane. With positive influences, our heart opens, our blood pumps faster, our energy increases. What is right for us uplifts; what is not right depletes us, and leaves us feeling let down.

Deep down most people seem to know more than they admit to. Learning to receive Inner Guidance is a matter of building on this inner knowing or intuition which everyone has if they but tune in to it.

CHAPTER 7.

INFINITE INFORMATION, HIGHER INTELLIGENCE

Once we learn to quiet our minds and to see with the mind's eye, we can perceive the more subtle and hidden aspects of our own thought process. We also can receive imagery from our deeper mind. In our peaceful "inner sanctuary," we may invite the God Within to speak to us. We also may call in information from all dimensions, including the Akashic Record, the Quantum Field, and telepathy with other beings. The fact is the firmament is one enormous information data bank. All *in-formation* is encoded in frequency patterns, all intertwined (entangled), holographically. Because of this, we are able to receive information from sources outside ourselves. The mind's eye is a gateway to many other dimensions. Assuming reasonably intact physical health, there is no information that cannot be accessed and cognized by the human mind, depending on the level of inner awareness of the individual, their pre-existing foundation of conceptual knowledge, and cognitive skills.

Another aspect of God that may be invited into the inner sanctuary is the Supreme Intelligence. God express him/her/itself through every molecule of one's being. Also it expresses itself as a Guiding Intelligence, *if* invited, and only if. At one point, while in inner silence, I asked if the Supreme Being intervened in human affairs. I received the following answer:

> "The overarching Intelligence that is the Almighty, the Creator, the Godhead, directs the overall evolutionary process, the evolution of the entire firmament. Divine Intelligence can alter certain thrusts of the vital life forces if they are too detrimental to the whole."

"Why, then," you might ask, "does He not alleviate the suffering of mankind, or prevent destruction of the very biosphere that sustains human life?" The fact is that we have free will, and the Creator does not interfere with that. When I asked specifically why the Supreme Being did not intervene to eliminate the very destructive genetically modified crops now being propagated by Monsanto and Sygenta and their allies in the US Government, this answer followed:

> "Nature is My chief way of determining what happens in the natural world. In the case of genetically modified plants, they are quite harmful to the integrity of natural plant DNA, but they also contain, if you will, the seeds of their own destruction. Because they lack Nature's intelligence in being able to adapt to variations in weather patterns, to withstand

drought, to develop natural resistance to pests, and to remain healthy in the face of these natural adversities, they will eventually die out. A direct interference by Me would upset the process of humans learning about the wisdom of nature."

In other words, Divine intervention is a "light touch." This exchange with the Divine took place in 2003, before super-bugs and superweeds appeared with a vengeance. As of this writing, we now are seeing that Monsanto's genetically modified (GM) cornstalks topple from root-worms devouring the roots of the stalks. Other pesticide-resistant superbugs and herbicide-resistant superweeds are are spreading at 'exponential' rates. [For more on GM crops, see Notes, page 198.]

It's never smart to accept anything on blind faith. What is here presented stems from what I've received and understand from my own experience. You must reach your own conclusions based only on what you yourself experience. Use your mind, your common sense and your discernment. Incorporate information available through ordinary sources. Do your homework, be alert and aware. Once you've done all you can by yourself, you can receive more help from Divine Guidance.

Several rich metaphysical experiences have proven to me that the "voice," my Inner Guidance, originates from a benevolent Source and Higher Intelligence, and not from my imagination. This has been demonstrated repeatedly. Here follows one example, that took place following my divorce in 1998.

I'd sold the house in Fairfax and moved to another lovely town in Northern California. There I first started the book publishing business, publishing for independent authors. In addition, I continued my spiritual journey. Given a dearth of authors in the area, my business was struggling. One mid-summer day I had run out of money. I didn't even have a dollar to buy food. As lunchtime approached the kitchen cupboard was literally bare. I had finished the last of the pasta that morning, and the preceding day I'd made the remaining few beef bouillon cubes into broth and polished it off. Now I was hungry.

I had experienced desperate hunger once before – and fortunately only once. It was instructive, to say the least. People act differently when they're very hungry. The experience, for me, was like having a wild animal inside me that had taken over and would do anything to have something to eat. I imagine the truly hungry person's craving for food can be at least as strong as a junkie's craving for his next fix. This time though, I was less trepidatious because I had more trust in Guidance.

Guidance was coming through now quite clearly. On this particular day, as lunchtime approached, my inner voice instructed me to take my daily walk. I started walking down the hill from my apartment to the town plaza – my typical daily walk. My usual route led around the right side of the tennis courts. As I reached the courts, the voice said, "Turn left." I did so, then walked the length of the courts, continuing toward the plaza. As reached the corner of the courts, the voice commanded, "Stop. Turn around." As I did, my eye fell upon something unusual amidst the thick bank of ivy growing alongside the sidewalk. A leaf of a grape vine peeked out from among the large dark green ivy leaves. I parted the leaves, and found a small grape vine, from which hung a full bunch of ripe purply-green grapes. This impressed me greatly, for I know that grapes do not grow in deep shade. Nor would a grapevine with sun-ripened fruit ever thrive beneath a dense cover of ivy.

I plucked the bunch of grapes. Every grape looked perfect and ripe, with a luminous quality about them – nothing other-worldly, but definitely noticeable. I returned home, rinsed the grapes, and ate every last one. They were delicious and perfectly satisfied my hunger.

This experience greatly mitigated any fear of ever having to go hungry. (Through Grace, industry or good fortune, I haven't since had to go hungry, except by choice when I've wanted to shed a few pounds.) I also was impressed by the practicality the Inner Guidance offered in directing me to food.

Inner Guidance has been and is extremely valuable to me. No detail is too small, no scope too large. I am daily guided in exactly what I need to eat to keep my body healthy. I've been directed unfailingly to where to seek my next job, both as an entrepreneur and in the corporate world. I must add here that the period of unemployment, proved necessary for my learning and growth. It forced me to consider carefully what I wanted to do next, and I was guided in how to train myself in new skills. I acquired new computer skills which prepared me to find work again. Unnerving though it was living with little or no money, I emerged from this period virtually unscathed.

I've continue to be guided where to find the right people I need to meet, where to find the exact tool I need for some household repair, or the exact article of clothing or book I might need. My inner voice has even presented me with original healthy recipes! It also has helped in doing dream interpretation, though earlier I had done my homework learning how this is generally done. I've used Inner Guidance to write business reports, books and poetry. Guidance also has helped me research various subjects in the social sciences and environmentalism.

Inner Guidance has become a reliable and trusted companion, a partner in co-creation. As a result of following Inner Guidance, my life is infinitely more rich, rewarding, and interesting than it would be without it.

The Quest for Higher Understanding

> *"He not busy being born is busy dying."*
> ~ Bob Dylan

I have always been hungry for knowledge, always sought to keep growing intellectually. For me, living by Guidance has been a journey of continual discovery and personal growth. Maintaining daily conversation with God is like having a watchful instructor who is there for me if I feel stuck, who course-corrects me if I wander into confusion. A terrific companion, God even makes me laugh if I'm blue. I'm never spoon-fed information, but am always helped if I need a nudge in the right direction. If I do my due diligence and can't find an answer from normal sources available to me, I ask Guidance for help. The fact is, we learn in steps, not all at once. One level of understanding is a stepping stone to the next. If information was dumped in our lap without prior research and inquiry, we wouldn't understand it because foundational knowledge would not be there.

Given the guidance and wondrous information I gained from connecting with Source, in 1999 I'd turned my life over to serving the Divine. I committed myself to strictly follow Guidance. Since then, my life has been more a co-creative partnership between my individual efforts and Divine Guidance. I have not had to struggle against the odds to make my way in the world. That said, life has not been all bliss and magic. I have faced many tests of faith, but none beyond my ability to pass. There have been moments of self-doubt. Still, I've stayed the course, usually because Guidance unfailingly beckons me onward, or dangles the proverbial carrot on a stick to keep me going.

Telepathy and Self-Realization

Because I am able to receive Guidance in the form of words and images, and can even receive long texts, including business writing, poetry, and non-fiction book text, I soon realized I could use the same mechanism to communicate telepathically with beings on this planet and from non-terrestrial locations. Why, you might ask, would anyone want to learn to connect with sources of information outside themselves? There are a number of reasons, the first of which is it is part of spiritual evolution.

In the Christian tradition, telepathy is considered one of the "gifts of Spirit." Mystics in other spiritual traditions view it as a sideshow at best, a parlor trick at worst. In the Buddhist and yogic traditions, telepathy is a "siddhi," an extended so-called occult power. Followers are discouraged from practicing it. Ramana Maharshi, for one, was hardly sympathetic. He deemed telepathy not worth striving for, saying this:

A man is possessed of limited powers and is miserable; he wants to expand his powers so that he may be happy. But consider if it will be so; if with limited perceptions one is miserable, with extended perceptions the misery must increase proportionately. Occult powers will not bring happiness to anyone, but will make him all the more miserable! Moreover what are these powers for? … Which is the real power? Is it to increase prosperity or bring about peace? That which results in peace is the highest perfection. (Godman 1985)

Maharshi warned of the danger of becoming attached to such powers as telepathy, that there is a strong temptation to let these powers inflate the ego rather than deflate it. For him, the desire for siddhis, or "super-natural" powers, and the desire for Self-realization were mutually exclusive. In Maharshi's view self-realization is the greatest attainment. Compared to that, telepathic powers are considered paltry.

And I would agree that this is so, if the individual has not done the baseline inner work of achieving and maintaining psychological and spiritual health, *and if* inner Self-realization is not the primary aspiration. Ramana Maharshi says that the self-realized person does not even have any desire for the siddhis. Once one attains Self-realization, one acquires all the "occult powers" in any case.

However, I would argue that at a certain stage of human evolution, becoming telepathic helps to connect one to a greater community beyond the self, and that as more and more humans acquire the ability to be telepathic, there will be much greater transparency among humans and thus less opportunity to lie and deceive. The existence of telepathy implies that we are all interconnected, as One. So inasmuch as we are all one, there should also result more compassion in the world. That is because if we are all one, we can experience others as ourselves, and thus our empathy is greatly extended. From empathy follows compassion. As scientist and mathematician Dr. Elizabeth Rauscher states,

> ... If there is, in fact, only one of us here in awareness, we should always choose compassion over justice, since we can always recognize compassion, but it is often difficult to discern justice from injustice. This is why the practice of compassion, and the teaching that separation is an illusion (nonlocality) are always found together in Buddhist writings. Compassion follows logically from life in a nonlocal universe. (Rauscher, Targ 2001)

The concept of Self-realization derives in large part from Eastern religions. In the Hindu religion self-realization refers to a profound spiritual awakening from an illusory self identity image (Ego), to the individual's true, divine, perfect nature. Some yogic traditions define self realization as a connection with your greater Self, or the first encounter with reality. Western psychology has added another dimension, emphasizing the fulfillment of the potential of one's personality. Psychologist Carl Rogers wrote of "the curative force in psychotherapy – *man's tendency to actualize himself, to become* *his potentialities...*to express and activate all the capacities of the organism." (Rogers 1961).

Abraham Maslow, an American professor of psychology, defined self-realization, which he termed self-actualization, as "the impulse to convert oneself into what one is capable of being." (Maslow 1968) In the early 1980's Western psychologists, myself included, began attempting to bridge the gap between Eastern philosophies, which de-emphasize the individual, and Western psychology, which places great importance on the development of the individual and "healthy ego." A healthy ego is considered the resilient interface between one's unique sense of self and the outer world – an interface that enables one to express fully his or her point of view, desires, needs, non-antagonistically, within the larger society. (Egoism, or egotism, on the other hand, is selfish in the negative sense. The egotist seeks superiority and domination over others, rather than cooperatively sharing his or her unique contribution to the common good.)

And so, what now may be our definition of Self-realization? In sixteen years of following Inner Guidance and opening to broader dimensions, I have come to understand that self-realization is not something one arrives at one day, suddenly achieving the state of "enlightenment." For years I sought to become enlightened, to finally arrive at a state where the workings of the universe would be revealed to me, and I'd have, perhaps, some bright light radiating from me, indicating I had made it at last. I based this vision on my belief that somebody somewhere had the true definition of enlightenment and that one day I'd come across it. To date, I haven't found anything definitive, though many sages are said to be enlightened. Even Christ and the Buddha must surely still be learning and evolving, wherever they are...

Each of us in our spiritual evolution and progression must be infinitely approaching the Godhead. My understanding is that there is only one absolute – the Godhead – and that It is pure energy. Until we become one with that Absolute Energy, perhaps *the* Absolute Intelligence, we are not yet "whole," but rather are ongoing works in progress. This evolutionary perspective is, to me, a thrilling, rather than a daunting perspective.

Chapter 8.

The Case for Telepathy

If you are to continue cultivating your inner vision be aware that it may lead to sensations and visions you could not imagine now. The tools of consciousness lead to the ability to see and do things that seem to violate the rules of life. Just as every garden in every year is different, and produces life you had not planned on and didn't see, so also does personal actualization involve recognizing senses you did not even know you had, and going ever deeper, just as a garden can become ever more ecologically complex.

What further reaches of human development are available to us if we continue our spiritual journey? For one, we can enhance our mental faculties. If properly nourished and stimulated, the human brain may continue to grow in adulthood, growing new neurons and forming new neuronal connections. (Dispenza 2007, Eriksson 1998, Kemperman 1999) That is, of course, if the individual isn't neglecting or abusing his or her physical health.

This returns us to the topic of telepathy. It follows that if we have opened to telepathic communication with all beings, including those of superior intelligence, then we can grow our own intelligence. (This is analogous to the idea that if you want to improve your tennis game, play with someone better than you.) A wise person, then, will opt to communicate with those who uplift and improve his or her understanding.

How Does Telepathy Work?

My theory is that telepathy probably works by the same mechanisms, or physics, as does Inner Guidance. It's just a matter of levels and of the particularities of the individual mind and baseline understanding. It is our natural birthright to maintain direct conversation with the Almighty, and so it is within the natural capacity of most of us to develop our telepathic abilities. I, for one, was not born with this ability. I had to develop it. You can do the same. This is not to say that you must be telepathic to receive uncannily brilliant communication from your deeper mind. Nor do you need to be telepathic in order to receive Inner Guidance.

To help you understand how this works – inner visioning, guidance, and telepathy – think of your mind's eye as being like a computer monitor. Your unconscious mind – your bio-hard drive, processes information and makes calculations. Your mind's eye shows you the results, like the computer monitor. Analogous to telepathy, your computer monitor can also show you information from the Internet, which has been processed by other computer hard drives.

The Internet is analogous to a "global brain" in its early "neural network" formation. It is conceivable that one day, fiber-optics as the nervous system of the Internet will be superseded by telepathic speed-of-light communications.

The mechanism by which the mind's eye receives images and words from the unconscious mind, via the pre-conscious mind, may differ from the mechanism of telepathy. Likely the difference is based on the fact that the physical brain uses bio-chemicals to convey the message, whereas telepathy may rely more on the holographic quantum field, the One Mind, that encompasses us all. One day science may demonstrate that pre-cognition, telepathy and clairvoyance rely less on bio-chemistry than on the "sea of information" contained within an interconnected, holographic, fractally encoded universe, or super-universe.

Scientific Evidence for Telepathy

In the early 1980's, I participated in classes to develop skills in clairvoyance. Each student was given a chance to clairvoyantly 'read' total strangers who had volunteered for the class as subjects. The overall accuracy of our readings was about 95%. We achieved the same rate of accuracy "reading" people having been given only a name, and only the instructor knew these people. Since that time, I have been immensely curious about how telepathy can be possible. Science now may be offering the beginnings of a satisfactory explanation.

When the US intelligence community learned that the USSR and China were conducting ESP research, our government became receptive to the idea of having its own competing psi* research program. (Schnabel 1997) From World War II until the 1970s the US Government occasionally funded ESP research. Their interest in ESP was for military purposes – remote viewing* of "enemy" targets. According to Schnabel, psychic spies, or "remote viewers," could infiltrate any target, elude any form of security, and never risk a scratch. For twenty years, the government trained civilian and military personnel for psychic ability, then put them to work full-time, at taxpayers' expense, against real intelligence targets. (Schnabel 1997)

Though the remote viewing program was officially shut down in 1995, it is possible the Government is still employing remote-viewers for military purposes. Even today, police departments hire people with well-developed extra-sensory abilities to help find missing people, bodies, murderers, etc.

Russell Targ's work of two decades of research at the Stanford Research Institute presents scientific support for remote viewing and the phenomenon of "nonlocality." Targ's data includes evidence from his work in training remote viewers for the US Government.

The *existence* of telepathy phenomena has been pretty well confirmed through many strict experiments. (Duane and Behrendt 1965) Nonetheless, much of the mainstream scientific community rejects remote viewing due to the absence of an evidence base they

---

*Remote viewing (RV) is the practice of seeking impressions about a distant or unseen target using paranormal means, in particular, extra-sensory perception (ESP) or sensing with the mind. Typically a remote viewer is expected to give information about an object that is hidden from physical view and separated at some distance.

consider sufficient, and to the lack of a theory which would explain remote viewing. In my view, though, there exist enough proven instances of significant experimental results to make ESP a valid field for further research and study. While the question of why and how telepathy actually works has not been adequately answered by mainstream science, current theories about quantum entanglement get us part way there. Quantum entanglement happens when the quantum energetic field of one person "entangles" with that of another for a period of time, during which thoughts and perceptions can be shared via telepathy. Dean Radin, PhD, a researcher in the field, sums up the situation in this way:

> Science is at the very earliest stages of understanding entanglement, and there is much yet to learn. But what we've seen so far provides a new way of thinking about psi.* No longer are psi experiences regarded as rare human talents, divine gifts, or "powers" that magically transcend ordinary physical boundaries. Instead, psi becomes an unavoidable consequence of living in an interconnected, entangled physical reality. Psi is reframed from a bizarre anomaly that doesn't fit into the normal world – and hence labeled paranormal – into a natural phenomenon of physics. (Radin 2006)

---

*The term psi denotes anomalous processes of information or energy transfer, processes such as telepathy or other forms of extrasensory perception that are currently unexplained by known physical or biological mechanisms. The term is purely descriptive.

Early theorists hypothesized that ESP could be explained by the fact of the brain's ability to propagate extremely low frequency waves (ELF's). "Low frequency" means there is a long distance between any two wave crests. When we are in a quiet, resting state, our brain waves are ELF. A resting human's brain waves range from 5 to 11 hertz, which are "extremely low frequency" wavelengths (ELF's). They're part of the basis for telepathy. (LoBuono 2010)

In the 1960s and 1970s there was intense interest in psi phenomena in the USSR. Distinguished Russian physicist I. M. Kogan advanced the concept that information transmission under conditions of sensory shielding was mediated by extremely low-frequency electromagnetic waves (ELF) in the wavelength region of 300 to 1000 km. The idea is that for separation distances of less than 1000 km, the percipient would still be in the induction field (near field) of the source, and would therefore experience less than inverse square fall off in signal strength. (Rauscher and Targ 2001)

LoBuono further explains this idea as follows:

> [As has been known for decades], long, low frequency waves can pass straight through the body of a human … and through other dense structures. Why? Because an atom is mostly just a void of seemingly empty space. The nucleus of an atom can be compared to a small, bizarrely fluctuating pea situated at mid-field in a large football stadium, while the electron would be a tiny micro-dot located way out in the furthest bleachers. So, energy waves can pass through an atom easily.

Ergo, energy waves can pass through the internal and external structure of your head, as well as the seemingly solid objects around you.

However, over distance, there is still a fall-off – the signal gets weaker and weaker. Some physicists, like Gerald Feinberg, propose that the carrier of the psi information could be the tachyon particle, which appears to travel faster than the speed of light. As he writes,

> This could allow one to experience a distant event before the corresponding light signal reached him, appearing to provide paranormal foreknowledge. However, the gain in temporal advantage would be only one nanosecond per foot of distance, whereas the data for precognition show that events are frequently described and experienced hours or days before the occurrence of an event. The advanced wave or tachyon would provide an hour's warning, only for events at a distance of 109 miles or greater. All electromagnetic or radio wave descriptions of psi suffer from these same limitations. (Rauscher and Targ 2011)

In light of experiments that have proven precognitive ESP (or "psi") – pre-cognitive information received days before an event – psi researchers and scientists currently favor the theory of quantum-interconnectedness and nonlocal correlations. Physicist David Bohm is a foremost proponent of this theory. He argues that we greatly misunderstand the illusion of separation in space and time. In his physics text book, *The Undivided Universe* (Bohm and Hiley 1993), he defuses this illusion as he writes about the quantum-interconnectedness of all things. Bohm says, "The essential features of the implicate order are that the whole universe is in some way enfolded in everything, and that each thing is enfolded in the whole." Physicist and parapsychologist Elizabeth Rauscher and Russell Targ, in explaining Bohm's theory of the holographic universe, write,

> ...the fundamental statement of the metaphor of the holographic ordering of the universe... says that, like a hologram, each region of space-time contains information about every other point in space-time. This model was inspired by the indications of nonlocality in Bell's theorem. And our data indicate that this information is available to our awareness. Bohm continues, '...all of this implies a thoroughgoing wholeness, in which mental and physical sides participate very closely in each other. Likewise, intellect, emotion, and the whole state of the body are in a similar flux of fundamental participation. Thus, there is no real division between mind and matter, psyche and soma. The common term psychosomatic is in this way seen to be misleading, as it suggests the Cartesian notion of two distinct substances in some kind of interaction.'
>
> In the holographic universe of David Bohm, there is a unity of consciousness, a 'greater collective mind, with no boundaries of space or time.' (Rauscher and Targ 2001)

As George LoBuono explained to me in private email correspondence, the whole story rests more in the realm of scalar wave forms:

"The new 'scalars' (also known as gravitics, electrogravity, and zero point energy) were the big step in seeing beyond the old Einstein limit." It is LoBuono's opinion that the unity of consciousness and remote mind communications are better described by a fractional kind of wave-form and mutual/universal resonance. (LoBuono 2011) Former U.S. Naval Surface Weapons Center physicist Eldon Byrd, PhD, is in agreement with the idea of scalar waves:

> I look at scalars strictly as information... Could it be that we live in a sea of information? Not in the form of electromagnetic energy, not acoustic energy, but a whole other form of energy which we currently have no instruments to measure. It's a sea of information. It's just there. It doesn't take any time for it to propagate from one point in time and space to another because it has nothing to do with time and space.
>
> A hologram is a scalar field; telepathic transmissions are holographic: A hologram results from the destructive and constructive interference of two superimposed coherent electromagnetic energy wave patterns. As a field of interference, a hologram is independent of direction and velocity. It is pure information. A hologram is also independent of space and time: illuminate a small portion of the hologram, and spherically distributed information of the whole is available in the part. A hologram is a scalar field. (Byrd 1991)

As Byrd further explains, "The production of synchronized, coherent electromagnetic energy by the human brain at a given frequency leads to a 'laser-like' condition increasing the amplitude and strength of the brain-waves. It also generates a scalar field containing the total 'information' of that individual." Another implication arises from this. Essentially, the more coherent our thinking, the more powerful our influence is on other people and in the world.

The Importance of ESP and Telepathy for Social Evolution

Is there value *other than* military applications, in developing and using telepathic abilities? According to my own experience, absolutely! Through telepathy, or ESP, one is able to connect with the intelligent universe in its myriad aspects – this multi-verse, peopled by beings of tremendous resources. Many inhabit advanced civilizations. If one is in harmony and has a firm commitment to acting in the interest of the "highest good," or "highest dharma," as Buddhists term it, then higher levels of knowledge become accessible. This can include telepathic information from more advanced civilizations elsewhere in the cosmos.

For example, a being from a civilization much older than our own, say, many thousands of years older than ours, may relate experiences that instruct or caution us against follies that may be foreseen, given the being's experiences on his or her own planet.

In 2002, a fellow medium and I received together a telepathic message from a being living on an unidentified planet. This being, a man, recounted that his own planet was turned into a vast desert, with hot white sand and blistering sun everywhere. This devastation occurred as a result of his people having clear-cut nearly all the forests and depleted their topsoil, which resulted in a cascade of further environmental degradations, including loss of freshwater supplies except that which could be obtained by seawater evaporation. Now the inhabitants lived in white tents on the desert and stayed alive only because their bodies had evolved to a more crystalline-based (silica-based) cell structure, rather than carbon-based, as humans on earth are. With this cellular transformation, they lived more as beings of thought, resonating to higher frequencies, nourished primarily by light frequencies. They still had solid form, though their bodies were much less dense than our own. While they were advanced mentally, physically they were incapable of producing much.

Widespread understanding and use of telepathy on earth would hasten our being accepted as full citizens of the multi-verse. Interplanetary citizenship is required if we, as earth inhabitants, wish to evolve past the limited confines of earth. It also would be helpful for anyone wanting to incorporate the higher understandings of advanced civilizations, for the purpose of applying them to earth existence. This is not to suggest there are not offenders in more advanced civilizations. Struggles between selfishness and thinking of the common good persist, as does the struggle against egotism, violations of ecological principles, and even the push for imperial colonization. However, gaining access to the intelligence, sciences and technologies of advanced civilizations might encourage us on earth to adopt less warlike, wasteful ways.

There are broad and vast implications of participating in an intergalactic community, both dangerous and beneficial. We must not proceed naively into this realm. Among the benefits that might be anticipated from communicating with beings from elsewhere in the galaxies, could be their sharing with us their advanced technologies. Already they have shared some of these. One of the people who've testified to this is Don Phillips, USAF, Lockheed Skunkworks design engineer. He says there are records and filmed documentation of meetings in California in 1954 between ETs and leaders of the USA. According to him, a few of the technologies we were able to develop because of the ETs include computer chips, lasers, night vision, bulletproof vests.... Phillips further testified that we not only have extraterrestrial devices but have also achieved tremendous technological advances from their study. (Disclosure Project Report 2001)

What kind of a world would we have if there were finally full disclosure by our government that we have been visited by beings from other planets, from advanced civilizations?

The Disclosure Project was formed in 2001 by American physician and ufologist, Steven Greer, and the resulting report includes the testimony of military and government witnesses to UFO/ET events, summaries of two major recent reports, and selected government documents. The purpose of the Project and report was to provide an overview of a public disclosure of the very complex UFO/ET (Unidentified Flying Object/ExtraTerrestrial) subject and to provide background materials and references for individuals to start their own research. As Dr. Greer writes,

Going back to the early 1950s, we have found that the basic technology and physics behind [these] ET spacecraft were discovered through very intensive reverse-engineering projects. … The basic physics behind the energy generation and propulsion systems were such that they could easily replace all existing energy generation and propulsion systems on the Earth. And with them, the entire geo-political and economic order.

The technological discoveries of the 1950s resulting from the reverse-engineering of extraterrestrial craft could have enabled us to completely transform the world economic, social, technological and environmental situation. That such advancements have been withheld from the public is related to the change-averse nature of the controlling hierarchy at the time – and to this day.

And make no mistake, the changes would be immense. Consider: A technology which enables energy generation from the so-called zero point field and which enables every home, business, factory and vehicle to have its own source of power – without an external fuel source. Ever. No need for oil, gas, coal, nuclear plants or the internal combustion engine. And no pollution. Period. (Greer 2001)

Ben Rich, the former head of Lockheed Skunkworks testified for the Disclosure Project, "We already have the means to travel among the stars, but these technologies are locked up in black projects and it would take an act of God to ever get them out to benefit humanity. Anything you can imagine we already know how to do." (Greer 2001)

Advanced so-called free energy technologies, seen as the Holy Grail of energy solutions – have been withheld by aliens, not just by the U.S. Government. Telepaths, including myself, have been told that human beings are still deemed too immature to handle these technologies responsibly. George LoBuono, whose telepathic abilities I believe to be very advanced, claims that aliens have long had technologies for "free energy," but they are well aware that there is a price to be paid for such access. There is no free lunch…. The aliens' concept of ecology is more comprehensive than our own, and includes considerations of over-population and the importance of not outgrowing the supply of natural resources, including the supply of energy. As LoBuono wrote in 2010,

> "Hyperversal aliens of much longer duration have repeatedly pointed out a further risk in the overuse of electrogravity and magnetogravity. Δt^* hyper-dynamics point to the fact that electrogravity ever so slightly shortens the duration of a universe cycle. Even though hyper-advanced aliens can minimize Δt locally, they can only do so at a total cost to a universe cycle's duration. This poses a dilemma for all aliens. To recklessly shorten the duration of an entire universe cycle would be irresponsible, hence, as humans are now beginning to learn, larger conventions regarding the use of negative-cycle technology appear to have been discussed – long before the appearance of human civilization." (LoBuono 2010)

Whether or not humanity will eventually become responsible enough to be permitted entry into the intergalactic community, individuals here can still use ESP to aid in their own development. As for broader social implications, for one thing, we are beginning to understand the applications of ESP for healing and growth, as in "remote healing."

Enticing though telepathy and clairvoyance may be, however, there are snares along the pathway to understanding the extra-sensory dimension, including individuals distorting ESP information due to their own unclarified, undisciplined, or egotistical subjectivity. Further, there is the delusional aspect: Many people believe they have experienced clairvoyance or intuition, when in fact these are products of imagination, frustration, fear, or ego. There are ways to correct for these missteps, however, and the reward for learning to use one's extra-sensory abilities are well worth the work it takes to clarify one's perception.

As with Inner Guidance, the first requirement for clarifying perception and receiving true clairvoyant or telepathic information is to achieve inner peace. There are no shortcuts for this. Attending a meditation class for six months and simply watching your thoughts pass is not enough. Thoughts and feelings must be understood, by identifying underlying false beliefs, how they originated, and then determining the accurate picture of reality. It is possible through sitting meditation,

---

*Note on Δt: "[Tom] Bearden goes so far as to re-state Einstein's famous equation as $E = \Delta t\ c2$. Scientists use the Greek symbol Δ (pronounced "delta") in equations to signify change. In other words, Bearden says that mass is equivalent to Δt (delta t), a change in time." (Bearden 1983)

like Vipassana, to reach Infinite Mind, from which true insight can arise. This requires long-term dedicated practice, though. For clarity, many people benefit from talking to someone else, perhaps consulting a trained professional, to gain more perspective than is possible in their isolated posture as a meditator.

Discernment

If you choose to develop your telepathic abilities and receive information from extra-sensory sources, it is advised that you exercise caution. You must be very careful to first identify with what or whom you are communicating. Discernment is critical. As Buddhists continually remind us, daily meditation is the key to gaining clear-mindedness, to letting superficial impressions and distorting interpretations to die away, revealing the core of perception underlying all. Such is the essence of discernment. Discerning individuals may rely on intuition, or their "gut feeling." However, until one has learned to distinguish true intuition from the distortions of desire, frustration or fear-based emotions, this can be tricky Emotion distorts perception and clouds true intuition. A person lacking in integrity will not have clear discernment.

One way to cultivate discernment is to pay attention to detail. The saying goes, the devil always hides in the details. Unfortunately, often there are many devils hiding there. Question the story line of any information you receive – whether from incarnate or non-incarnate beings. Note any inconsistencies, contradictions, and factual details that seem questionable.

Finally, always require those sending you information to identify themselves. If they refuse, walk away. They are not acting on your behalf. If they claim to be the Holy Virgin, or Christ Michael, the late Pope John Paul II, St. Germain, Mary Magdeleine, Qwan Yin, or a representative of the so-called "Galactic Federation," or any other of these unimpeachable-sounding names, don't accept it at face value. Even if you hear that the beings are "angels" or "spirit guides," be sure you know with whom you are communicating. The devil wears many clever disguises. (The term "devil" here refers to any number of forms of evil – knowingly doing harm, whether in small or large ways, or through supporting with the harmful designs of others.)

To ensure that the information you receive truly originates from the Creator, or whatever term suits your particular cosmology, always precede any meditation or session in mediumship by clearly stating that all information must come only from the highest source. You might, for example, write, say or mentally express the following: "I require that any information I receive come only from the highest source. So be it." Powerful though this statement is, the capacity for human self-deception is great and may at times override this pure intention.

George LoBuono concurs with the need for discernment and offers additional insights:

> You must first become skilled at noting the difference between your subtly and gently inter-dimensioned thoughts, versus your thoughts that have a nearly audio-like verbal character. Some of your thoughts are framed in terms of how they might later be spoken, while others

are more complex and may converge from a number of different internal perspectives. Once you see the difference between the two, you will know your own internal tenor. Thoughts communicated by an external source may have a more audio-like, verbal character. They may diverge from your accustomed way of thinking, hence they are out of character. They stand out." (LoBuono 2010)

Quantum physicists have started offering sound explanations for how information can be accessed non-locally. Experiments testing non-local healings have been proven effective in certain cases. But thus far, quantum physicists have not tackled the issue of discernment in more than a superficial way. In controlled tests of remote viewing, scientists have occasionally identified clues that would "tip off" the subject. Naturally, this invalidates both the test and the results.

Information received non-locally, apart from what can be shown in diagrammatic form, is subject to the interpretation by the perceiver, or the medium. Every individual has his or her own unique filter for information, be it a clarified filter or one clouded by unconscious fears, false beliefs, desires, or fear-based emotions. Immature or uneducated minds are unable to comprehend information from more advanced sources except in ways that match the receiver's mental abilities. The lack of mental sophistication does not, however, preclude someone receiving different types of "knowingness," such as intuition or a "felt sense." Peasant cultures abound with individuals with advanced spiritual awareness. Many shamans, medicine men, and tribal leaders are able to leash "unseen" forces for spiritual and physical healing.

Generally, even Western psi researchers have yet to consider the issue of discernment in regard to the influences that may come through different types of non-terrestrial beings. Ego distortions, so rife on the earth plane, also exist in other dimensions. Non-embodied beings can be malicious, manipulative, deceiving, or simply mischievous. Some are benign, even reliable. Naiveté also exists among human souls who've "crossed over," who may possess great integrity but limited understanding. Because of this, telepathic messages and other forms of mediumship must be treated with great discernment.

We in the modern world are deluged by information overload. This is increased by orders of magnitude when accessing the evolving digital electronic network, the Internet. In addition, we are seeing heightened intuitive abilities in a growing number of people. This is occurring in part because of the electronic network, the "Infosphere," or "Global Brain," as some have termed it. There is a ladder effect – by raising awareness, the global electronic information network dispels illusions precipitated by insufficient information. As a result of increased awareness, many more individuals are accessing the "quantum mind," as physicist-philosopher Amit Goswami dubs it. This field of encoded energy signals surrounds us and permeates our being. Information becomes accessible non-locally; distance no longer matters. By tapping into the quantum mind, we penetrate the "Veil," such through clairvoyance and telepathy communication can be initiated with non-terrestrial and non-incarnate beings.

The quantum mind might also be seen as the "All That Is," the "One Mind," "Highest Dharma," or God, depending on your philosophy or theology. It does not matter what you call it. What is important is how you use it.

The spiritual journey, in my opinion, is one of continual progress toward clarifying the soul's purpose. Nothing endures outside of this. Life presents us with one transitory experience after another, until one day, or one lifetime, or one eon, we experience the Absolute, the All That Is, which, as a modest definition of the Godhead, is pure, sentient, creative, intelligent light. Until that time, we continue on our way, cultivating deeper understanding that the interplay of light and forms in our world is but a mirror for us, designed to teach us that appearances are infinitely mutable and subject to collective and individual creative forces. Now and forever we create, add weight or variation to consensual reality, whether consciously or unconsciously. So be careful. Use the intelligence you are gifted with to its fullest. And, above all, stay aware.

Subtle Dimensions of Reality

Reality, if it is to be defined, is comprised both of variables and constants. The constants are defined by the laws of physics. These are only partially understood by modern-day physicists, even by quantum physicists. For centuries philosophers have been polarized between the idealist and the materialist world views. Idealists claim that ideas are the prime mover of reality; the materialists say matter is all that matters. The bridge between the two likely is found in the laws of physics and in our growing understanding of physics.

That which was once seen as "solid," now is viewed by physicists as mutable and ever-changing. Physics teaches us that everything is in a process of becoming and dying. You grow and evolve, unless you are out of alignment. When you are aligned and in harmony, your innate potential for evolutionary growth is optimized.

Reality is also an ongoing, shifting process, although the laws of physics are constant. The *I-Ching*, or *Book of Changes*, a classic Chinese text, teaches that any partial aspect of reality, once fully experienced, leads to its opposite. This can be seen at the individual level as well as at the level of society. The same principle is stated in the law of the unity of opposites. We cannot hold onto a fragment of reality and expect it to remain unchanged. Only if we are aware of the whole and the continual balanced process of change can we avoid being buffeted from one polarity to the other. The more we see what is, rather than what we wish, the better able we are to maintain our balance.

Reality for most of us is made up of the day-to-day events that contribute to our becoming who we are. Such events and occasions change over time, and as they do, so ideally do we. This view of reality is purely subjective. An increasing number of scientists now agree that reality is not static, and that there are few constants. They further acknowledge that the universe is expanding and that the basis of physical existence is an ever-changing process. Astrophysicist Paul LaViolette, PhD, has formulated a cosmology of subquantum kinetics. This posits a new view of our cosmos as an open, order-generating universe, continuously creating matter and energy. It predicts a new form of energy, continuously emerging within all planets and stars.

LaViolette's approach is consistent with the ideas of Albert North Whitehead, mathematician, philosopher and logician, who was familiar with the quantum physics of the 1920's. A proponent of process philosophy, Whitehead postulated that everything in the universe is characterized by experience (which is not to be confused with consciousness); there is no mind-body duality under this system, because "mind" is simply seen as a very developed kind of experiencing. La Violette's theory is also consistent with the concepts of physicists Louis de Broglie and Richard Feynman.

Instead of considering the particles of matter as closed systems, subquantum kinetics conceives only of open systems, ever exchanging particles and energy with the surrounding environment. LaViolette's concept of open systems extends to the whole universe, considering it infinite in extent and probably of eternal duration. (LaViolette 2010). Many of his predictions from his subquantum kinetics methodology have been verified by observations through the Hubble Space Telescope. (LaViolette 1985-1997) This implies, if not proves, that we are all part of one big evolutionary process. For those of us who need science to assure us that we can grow and change, and that we have perhaps infinite potential, the science is now there.

CHAPTER 9.

ALIGNING WITH OUR TRUE NATURE

Each of us has the ability to envision and create the life we want, in spite of seemingly insurmountable obstacles. All we imagine can come to be. In God's imagination, we are projected through light, *qua* color, into space-time. So in imagining your desired life, you are engaging in a God-like act. Your imagination can project vibrations into the temporal realm and produce effects.

Alignment and Harmony

We might think that contemplating the life we desire is indulging in idle fantasy. Or we might consider it utopian to seek a world in which we might exercise all of our innate capabilities. But the fact is, by clearly envisioning what we truly desire in our heart we come into greater alignment with our soul and our innate design for realizing our full potential. On the subtle level, by envisioning our deepest desires we activate the vibrational harmony of our particular being. Once you harmonize yourself with your soul, then it can align with higher organizational principles, all within the grand design of the firmament. Such alignment brings coherent focus and personal power to our work, aspirations and actions.

What about someone, you might ask, who envisions having a grand castle in which to enjoy splendid isolation, fine décor and magnificent views of the countryside? Such a vision might be seen to be inspired merely by greed and selfishness. But this is not necessarily the case. This person may be using this imagined scenario to align himself with the inner ordering principles of his soul essence. There is an element of the monastic in this vision: it may be helping him see himself as whole unto himself, not dependent on others for his wants and needs. Such endeavor can be a wholesome activity, or it can fall into a negative version of selfishness.

Because the soul contains the perfect template for our individual material form, when we harmonize with our unique soul essence through imagination or vision, we align with All That Is.

Harmonic Levels

The principle of harmony states that if one removes confusion and mistaken belief system, and if one attains a state of peacefulness such that the mind is no longer fragmented in incoherent thinking, darting about here and there, then one opens the doorway to the Infinite. Inner nature corresponds to outer nature, within us and throughout the universe. The holographic view is valid: All That Is is enfolded into every cell, every molecule of our body. No need to question the nature of the Creator – everything in the universe – or multi-verse, may be known by direct perception. Unfortunately, many humans are ensnared by occluding thought forms acquired during several lifetimes (assuming there are many lifetimes or incarnations). Until they achieve the peacefulness that comes with a quiet mind, they will not be able to cognize the directives from Source.

Levels of Awareness

The more aligned we are with our deepest nature, our unique soul essence, the more we optimize our individual potential for perfection. There are levels and levels of awareness we may achieve through going within and doing our inner spiritual work. Crumbling in the face of opposition isn't what is meant by "going within." It is, rather, a way to attain a greater alignment with the harmony and balance inherent in the architecture of the firmament. The higher one's level of awareness and alignment, the greater is one's level of understanding, feeling of peace, and sense of the unity of all things, and the greater is one's effectiveness as an actor on the stage of life.

As we bring ourselves into harmony with our own deepest nature, we achieve what may be known as a harmonic level. Once attained, a harmonic level holds. There are many harmonic levels, as one ascends the ladder of soul development. Each echelon, or grouping of harmonics, has its particular range of influence. One's harmonic level affects the quality of his or her life. Say you have achieved a level of 100 or more on a scale of 10 million levels of elevation available to humans. *[author's note: the 10 million levels is a number I received through channeling, from Source.]* At the level of 100 your soul vibration is sufficiently powerful to overcome most dualities. You are able to supersede the dichotomy of good and evil within yourself. More specifically, people at that level and beyond are assured that an "evil" vibration will simply be resolved within his or her own auric field (the field occupied by the aura), such that a manifestation of "evil" or "bad" may never enter the equation. If in the past you have been attacked on any level of your being by "enemies," once you achieve level 100 and beyond, you need never more fear this. Your life, then, becomes a dance, in which the protagonist and antagonist engage in ever more refined levels of interaction.

The levels between 100 and 12,000 are experienced as a gradual "lightening" of the being. This may be felt as increasing levels of energy, intelligence, buoyancy and cheerfulness, delight in being alive, effortless forbearance when confronted by the discomfort or pain of others, increasing insight, sustained equanimity, and a greater appreciation for the orderliness of the Cosmos, despite appearances of chaos at the lower levels.

Proceeding forth in spiritual evolution, at level 12,000 one begins to experience the presence of inner light. It isn't what has been termed "enlightenment." It is, rather, a feeling of being suffused with a subtle and warm luminescence. (Those practicing pranayama breath techniques may experience this on a transitory basis.) Such light is less intense than in moments of rapture which are experienced occasionally in the early stages of spiritual ascent. A continuing state of rapture, in the sense of ecstasy, isn't a goal to be striven for, in my opinion, lovely though it is. One cannot operate in an interconnected world if one is melted in a puddle of light all the time.

On attaining a level of 12,000, one may feel overwhelmed at first, or, in common parlance, "blissed out." To maintain one's ground of understanding, it is important to hold a clear view of the ultimate orderliness of the firmament. A person who lacks such appreciation may become lost in striving for ever more pleasing states of bliss. This seems counterproductive, for the reason one works to clarify one's being is to achieve peace, harmony and beauty. If bliss is in the mix, it comes as an extra.

The way one achieves these levels is through the ongoing practice of meditation. In the stillness of meditation, one may connect to All That Is and gradually open to increasingly powerful energies from the Cosmos. These energies move one up the scale. All one need do is be still and receive.

Chaos versus Order

Perception depends on the level from which you are observing things. What we see happening in the world (the local level), and what we experience in relationship to that may be very chaotic. If, however, we take a higher perspective, we begin to see patterns. At an even higher perspective, we see increasing levels of orderliness.

The higher one ascends in understanding and awareness, the more one resonates with the cosmos. As with the holograph, the whole of Creation contains all else; we are all contained within a vast quantum field. Order exists at higher levels, with supreme order reigning at the highest level. At the lower levels, however, we may experience chaos. That is because pure energy is stepped down as it becomes dense matter, and in so doing, becomes increasingly chaotic, by degrees. The local level is the most chaotic, being a very dense array of dense material. Here we have what quantum physicists have observed at the microscopic level as being what they term a "violent quantum foam." Physicist Brian Greene writes,

> Going in reverse order [away from the quantum foam], from the near to the more distant, the random, violent small-scale undulations cancel each other out – in much the same way that, on average, our compulsive borrower's bank account shows no evidence of his compulsion – and the concept of a smooth geometry for the fabric of the universe once again becomes accurate. It's like what you experience when you look at a dot-matrix picture: From far away the dots that compose the picture blend together and create the impression of a smooth image whose variations in lightness seamlessly and gently change from one area to another. When you inspect the picture on finer-distance scales you realize, however, that it markedly differs from its smooth, long-distance appearance. It is nothing but a collection of discrete dots, each quite separate from the others. (Greene 1999)

Rather than despair, believing the world is self-destructing, that Shiva, the Goddess of Destruction, is destroying all form, it serves to remember that there are higher ordering principles. Out of chaos, new designs emerge. When chaos becomes extreme, higher orders of self-organization emerge. As Professor Christopher Bache, Professor of Religious Studies at Youngstown State University and adjunct faculty member at the California Institute of Integral Studies, writes,

> Chaos theory tells us that when a system is driven beyond equilibrium, the subtle interconnectedness that lies latent beneath its surface can sometimes emerge to reshape the system itself. In his well-known study of dissipative structures, Ilya Prigogine has shown that one of the properties of far-from-equilibrium systems is their capacity for higher self-organization. When driven into far-from equilibrium conditions, some systems do not just break down; they generate new structures that pull higher forms of order out of the surrounding chaos. It is as if nature reaches into herself and draws forth higher orders of self-organization that are latent within the system, hidden and quiescent until their potential is actualized. (Bache 2000)

The Octets and the Unified Field

According to channeled information I received from Source, there exists a fundamental ordering principle of the cosmos. The architecture of the firmament is based upon the principal of octaves. The octaves are orderings of light and sound frequency patterns. The patterns comprise wave and particle aspects as well as sub-atomic aspects, including those not yet measurable by our science. In seeking to elevate one's awareness one strives to rise (or be raised) to higher levels in the structure of the octets.

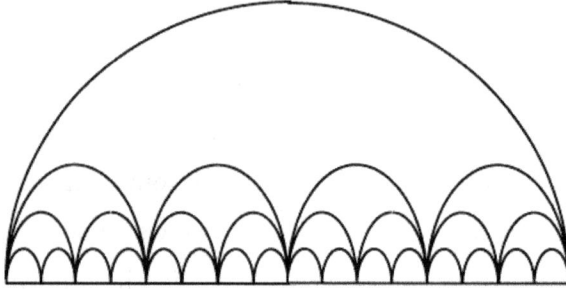

In the drawing above, the lower echelon, or set, represents the incidental and accidental effects of nature. The second level (or octet), represents a level in which order is imposed by the Divine. You might ask, isn't nature already "ordered"? Well, yes and no. Nature has its own intrinsic ordering principle – often in conflict with humankind. When animals and nature cohabitate alone, they harmonize and blend as if by Divine ordering. When human civilization comes into play, more often it carves its mark into the biosphere and disturbs rather than blends with nature. Thus, clash ensues. The third echelon in this drawing represents future potential.

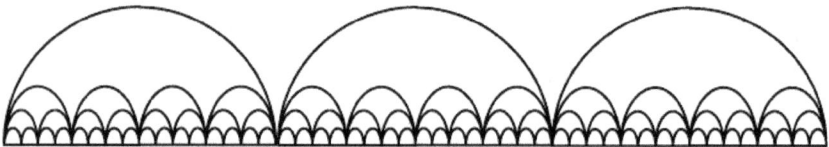

These three sets may be brought into harmonious balance by an even higher octaval grouping. Thus, three sets are bridged by a single over-arching set, as illustrated below, which harmo-nizes all notes on the scale, so to speak. The octet is one ordering. There also are groupings of 10, 12, 15, etc., *ad infinitum*. Each grouping has a characteristic frequency. Frequency harmonics can have the aspect of light and color, as well as the aspect of the sound wave, or tone.

Several octaval arrangements may in turn be harmonized by another overarching grouping:

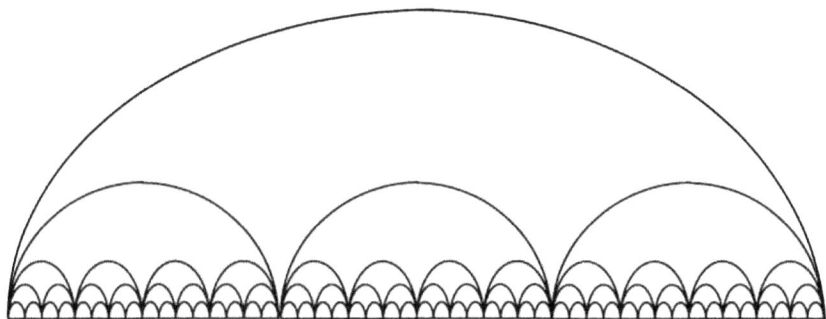

The Aspect of Sound

The aspect of tone, or sound, is perhaps easier to understand than light frequency. Tone involves the harmonious blending of scales – a range of notes. For example, take the blending of a pentatonic scale (five notes) with an octaval scale (eight notes). This is only achieved within a scale that is the multiple of both of these. So, 5 x 8 = 40. However, 40 cannot be reduced and still be divisible by both 5 and 8, so we need the 40-tone scale.

"What about a 15-tone scale and a pentatonic scale?" one might ask. A higher ordering has to be a multiple of the two scales in question. So, in this instance, we need only a 15-tone scale, because

15 is divisible both by 15 and 5. A 15-tone scale could comprise both the pentatonic scale and the 15- tone scale.

On the other hand, an 8-tone scale cannot be comprised within a 75-tone scale, because 75 is not a multiple of 8.

To harmonize an octaval scale with a pentatonic scale and a 15-tone scale, multiplying, 5 x 15 x 8, we get 600. However the overarching scale can be 120, as 120 is evenly divisible by each of these numbers. A 120-tone scale can harmonize our three scales. The mathematics considered above may all be subsumed vibrationally, that is, contained within the vibrational frequency pattern of an individual or whatever entity we are considering.

The Aspect of Color

Color contains its own vibration. A particular color may hold a frequency value of, say, 120, equating to our musical scales above. The color might be lavender, a red-violet, in all shades. The darker shades represent the more fixed pattern, which is capable of organizing the most unstable of the elements in an octet, or a ten-part group, or quintet, etc. This is analogous to the lower rung of the first drawing, the accidental, coincidental, and chaotic elements.

The lighter shades hold the higher frequencies within the vibratory field, such that a very upsettable person in the lavender group may require the deeper hues to organize and stabilize him- or herself, while a very highly evolved human in the ray may only require a light shade of the palest lavender to contain him or her in his optimal alignment.

Scientific studies show that color can impart a sense of peace and harmony to an individual, and even in a social setting. On the personal level, if one identifies a specific color that induces calmness, say, one might choose that color in clothing and décor. It is also possible during meditation to absorb the chosen color frequency into one's being by gazing at a swatch of paper or fabric of that color. Focus on that swatch for twenty minutes. Envision the color filling the body: first the head, then shoulders and arms, chest, and on down to the feet. Hold the vision as long as possible. If you want to feel refreshed after an unpleasant encounter, you might envision a lemon yellow color filling your body. Deep purple-blue (akin to the last light fading from the sky) might grant you access to the deep space beneath chaotic impressions. Pearly white light may bring you powerful inner renewal.

All of life – plants, animals, and humans – is held in a web of vibratory frequencies. By attuning to these frequencies we increase our levels of harmony and balance, and so bring ourselves progressively into a closer relationship with the Creator. The benefits are many. The more aligned we are, the more smoothly our life flows, our health improves, and we receive increasingly elevated and accurate information from Source.

The more aligned our consciousness, the greater its coherence. As consciousness reaches a higher level, a unified field, it helps manifest the potential and possibilities of the individual. So, in addition to resonating at a level that brings you desirable persons and outcome, you yourself become a creator. If an individual is a high enough creator, he or she can set the tone for what is around them, such that like-minded individuals will be attracted. Collectivities have exponentially more creative power than the power of one.

The garden of the world erewhile,

Thou Paradise of the four seas

Which Heaven planted us to please,

But, to exclude the world, did guard

With wat'ry if not flaming sword;

What luckless apple did we taste

To make us mortal and thee waste!

Unhappy! shall we never more

That sweet militia restore,

When gardens only had their towers,

And all the garrisons were flowers;

When roses only arms might bear,

And men did rosy garlands wear?

~ Andrew Marvell

Chapter 10

Imagination, Creativity, Intuition, and Changing Reality

Image and Illusion

Many of us limit our concept of reality to that which we can see, feel and touch. These are fixed components, we think, and we don't challenge them until they begin to seem inadequate. However, what we know about reality is, in fact, conditioned by what we are taught to believe. Reality is largely indefinable, because it is constantly evolving and changing. If we limit our view of reality to what is tangible, we are cut off from the ever-shifting forces which underlie all appearances.

Any appearance of solidity is largely a construct of the mind – a projection into a mutable field, coming from one's own perspective or point of view. When a group or a society shares the same point of view, we have a consensus reality, which appears to be even more solid or immutable. But everything is mutable; the basis for creating any material manifestation lies within our imagination, our perceptions, our subjective world of ideas, desires and designs.

"We might call imagination the stimulating principle of the mind. It is that which unifies the various aspects of sensible intuition."

~ George Seidel, *The Crisis of Creativity*

Imagination as Conscious Design

Imagination can be a precursor for action: it can create designs for real solutions. We can consciously direct imagination toward practical ends. We create what we want in imagination before we manifest it. Just as an architect envisions a design before he makes a drawing, just as a composer hears music in his imagination before he writes it down, so we imagine how we want our lives to be before we make plans for action. Imagination allows us to envision alternatives to any given reality and so set the course of action to realize those alternatives. In this way we free ourselves from the strictures or determinations of our condition.

Now more than ever we have the ability and tools for envisioning and designing scenarios, plans, programs and products – any required information, protocol and research are at our fingertips, via the Internet and other electronically-enabled forms of instant communication.

Intuition

Intuition differs from imagination in that it is not created, but received. Intuition presents solutions or insights we receive in our mind's eye, or in our gut in the form of a deep knowingness. Such intuition usually comes after we have researched or applied our conscious understanding to a specific problem or issue. Then we allow time for the unconscious mind to process our conscious input. In moments of stillness we may receive an answer which takes into account not just our research, but also relevant information from our unconscious mind.

Intuition is a powerful ally that frees us from logically having to figure everything out. Our job is to take charge of our lives as best we can. But after doing all that we know to do, more help can come to us. The more relaxed and free from worry we are, the more open we are to intuition, inspiration and opportunity.

It important to understand imagination and intuition, for both faculties enable us to live our highest calling, or purpose, in life. Once we envision a desired goal in imagination, our intuition can shepherd us along the path to its fulfillment. In fact, intuition is the gateway to guidance from a Higher Power.

Inspiration

Inspiration is intuition that comes in a rush. And it leaves us as quickly as it comes. To make use of inspiration, we must have ready a medium for its expression. If we don't channel it, it may be lost. But if our mode of expression – our art or our craft – is well honed, we can use inspiration for almost any creative application.

Keeping alive the creative spirit keeps us from succumbing to conditioning, to conventions that don't suit us and are stifling. Depression, so widespread in our culture, often results from individuals stifling their creative spirit, and instead conforming to society in ways that do not support their inherent natures.

Each of us has the capacity to receive inspiration, to express our unique gifts, to express our contribution in a way that may not have been done before. This is creativity in its multi-faced form. Our innate creative spirit requires that we identify what we passionately care about, then develop a vehicle for its expression. This can take many forms: writing, fine art, music, craftsmanship, and even the art of relationship, statesmanship, or visionary reformation. Once identifying our passion, we must devote ourselves wholeheartedly to understanding and cultivating its expression. When the groundwork is laid, inspiration fills us and pulls from all of our unique knowing. We are inspired then to express our gifts in totally unique ways.

Creative geniuses often talk about their inspiration as coming in a rush. Goethe, Brahms, Henry Miller and Andre Breton, for example, all said that after they prepared their craft they tuned to the cosmos for the creative spark. Author and playwright Henry Miller said, "Who writes the great books? It isn't we who sign our names. What is an artist? He's a man who has antennae, who knows how to hook up to the currents which are in the atmosphere, in the cosmos." (Brewster 1985)

Goethe said of certain of his poems, "I had no picture of them, no advance idea; they fell unexpectedly into my mind and wanted to be set down at once, so that my impulse was to jot them down wherever I found myself, instinctively and as though in a dream." (Ghiselin 1985)

The importance of creative spirit transcends the realm of the personal. Only by assuming our rightful roles as creators can we envision new strategies and designs for the continued evolution and survival of the human species. We have witnessed the enormous destructiveness of warfare, ecological disaster, economic chaos, and extreme forms of personal alienation that have plagued the late twentieth and early twenty-first century. At this critical point in our social evolution, it is essential that we envision a new social order.

If humanity is to survive, it is essential that we harness the joint powers of imagination and creativity. Beyond art and invention, these powers must now be applied to the solution of problems in the body politic, in technology, and in systems for human sustenance. The good news is that given these gifts, if we get beyond limited thinking and beliefs we can achieve whatever we truly want for our own good and that of the larger order.

Authenticity

While I am not an artist, *per se,* I consider my life and work to be a creative process. In the beginning of my work years I changed jobs frequently because my interest in these positions waned within a year or so. Still, each job helped me learn skills and to identify my strengths, talents, what I liked to do, and what I cared about. Using this knowledge, eventually I was able to design my own career. Through a process of elimination, I was able to identify what I cared about. Anything I felt lukewarm about was tossed out. This helped clarify my vision.

Each time I re-invented my career, I had to identify what I truly cared about at that particular stage of my life. At the outset I didn't know what I was aiming for, however by the time I found it, it had a shape and sense all its own. And it worked. It had potency because it was a coherent expression of who I am.

When I started my psychotherapy practice, my motivating interest was to understand and encourage the creative process itself. I wanted to live in a society of inspired people, ablaze with their unique intelligence and understanding, contributing their unique gifts to the whole. I had experienced this briefly in the heyday of post-hippie Berkeley, where I lived after graduating from Stanford University in Palo Alto. For awhile, small neighborhood communities were so full of love and inspiration that people didn't even need much sleep! We had food co-ops, poetry, music, love, and more inspiration than could be contained in any one form of expression. This was a rare, and unfortunately fleeting moment.

I wanted this moment to be ongoing throughout society, in some form or other. Toward that end, I specialized in understanding what prevented people on the personal level from living inspired lives. For my learning, and to serve, I focused my psychotherapy practice on helping blocked writers become unblocked. What was common to all of these blocked creatives was that they had never asked themselves what they really cared about. Most had been conditioned to believe that indulging in such fantasy would be selfish. Once I explained that this was the one and only way to access their creativity, once I showed them how to get in touch with what they truly cared about, their creativity sprang forth anew. (McChrystal 1980)

Creativity is not some special gift bestowed exclusively on artistic geniuses. Our creative contribution comes from our willingness to be, say and do what we truly think, feel and want. Each of us is unique; we each bring to life a unique perspective. Expressing this is a creative act, because no one else has ever expressed it before.

CHAPTER 11.

CONSUMERISM AND POWER

Many people have been captured by the lures of consumerism in our commodified society, where everything has been turned into a commodity to be purchased, including art, music, sexual stimulation, any small satisfaction of instinctual energy. This is all designed to keep us passive, out of touch with our own creativity and expression of who we really are. Consumerism is, in short, repressive.

Herbert Marcuse, German philosopher and co-founder of the Institute for Social Research, wrote extensively and critically about the commodified society. He maintained that mass media, advertising and corporate management work together to quell opposition to the dominant system of production and consumption. In such a society, one of the primary means of domination is repressive desublimation. (Sublimation is defined as turning basic instinctual energy into a more "sublime" or refined expression or satisfaction.) The commodified society permits some degree of natural expression or satisfaction of instinctual energy through the consumption of commodities, but this serves to dampen any demands of its citizens for the freedom to lead genuinely satisfying lives. (Marcuse 1991. See also Notes: Marcuse, "Desublimation.")

People who live as mere consumers are cheating themselves. By acquiescing to a life of mere consumption, people deny themselves the genuine satisfaction that comes from living authentically, expressing their full creative spirit. In the context of a commodified society, creativity has the power to radically transform the self as well as society. By radical, I mean "going to the root or origin; fundamental," that is, it can make a radical difference.

From sublimation come sublime satisfactions! Keeping alive the creative spirit enables one to live an inspired life. When people are inspired, fear vanishes. Suddenly individuals regain the power to move mountains, so to speak. We have seen how creative people can be when finally they say they've had enough abuse, as in the case of the Spring 2011 uprisings throughout the Middle East. In the Fall of 2011, the Occupy movement started with just nineteen protestors in New York City. Within a month it had become international, all because people joined together to protest political and financial abuses that had become intolerable and had endured too long.

But when the forces of oppression are not so obvious, and they insidiously grow stronger, we may find ourselves dying by degrees, like the frog being slowly boiled to death... Keeping the creative spirit alive keeps us out of hot water!

On Power and Domination

The will to power and domination over other human beings can be seen as a failure of creativity at the fundamental level. Animals use power and domination rituals as their only means of survival and successfully competing for resources. They are not creative (with a few exceptions), and thus have no alternative. Humans have the inherent ability to invent solutions to problems, to contribute to life-enhancing activities for the greater society. They do not need to dominate.

Dominators seek to hold on to what they know; what gives them security is based only in authority, legitimate or not, and usually illegitimate. They do not usually see themselves primarily as positive creators, as contributors to the greater society. Those who seek power over others usually are found, consciously or unconsciously, to feel unimportant and undeserving. Rather than identifying the source of pain and doing the inner work to heal themselves, instead they grab for power over others as a consolation. By making others feel small, they themselves gain the sense that they are big.

Sadly, the lack of self esteem, the sense of feeling inadequate, prevails no matter how impressive the façade of wealth and power might be. Despite superficial appearances, this person simply cannot acknowledge his true worth as a human being.

The will to power and domination is not confined to the male of the human species. Women who have climbed up the rungs of the power structure to become either part of the managerial class or the elite can become equally domineering, just as captured by the lure of wealth and power over others as are the men.

Beyond male (or female) domination over others, beyond designated categories of left and right, conservative, liberal and neo-liberal, beyond categories of capitalism, socialism or mixed-economies, there is the force of creativity – the life force itself.

A radically creative spirit aligns itself with the evolutionary thrust and aspirations of humankind. Being "radically" creative means using the life force not as mere instinctive activity, nor simply to propagate the species, but moreover to manifest higher levels of human evolution, of social organization, and to further develop human potential. If individuals are in touch with their creative spirit, they will rise above the reactionary patterns of domination and submission.

People who fixate on having power over others are not in touch with their heart's desire, and so lose touch with their creativity in any positive sense. Heart's desire, in this instance goes deeper than fleeting sensual pleasures or the satisfaction of amassing wealth. True heart's desire is based in the heart's ability to love self and others. The capacity to love expands outward to the larger sphere, to envisioning a planet of abundance and beauty for all. True heart's desire recognizes that one cannot be happy in isolation, that if there is misery surrounding one, it will be felt by the loving heart, an empathic heart. And, so, energy will go toward relieving misery, toward working to attain the highest good for all. In this, one gains the deepest satisfaction and begins to access the true meaning of life.

If we think we need power over others, we need to look deeper. We rightly want to feel powerful, but we will derive greater satisfaction by using our personal power to do good, rather than making others feel small and subservient. Recognizing and accepting our own personal power allows us love more effectively. Everyone wants to love and be loved, for who we truly are.

Our personal vibrance and effectiveness expand when we express and involve ourselves in that which we truly love. This calls forth our inner resources and focuses them creatively. We work from the best we have to offer and thereby make ourselves, and those with whom we associate, stronger. In the process, our personality takes shape and matures.

Skillful Relationships

The single most powerful vehicle for spiritual growth is the human relationship. We can learn much about our relationships with others by turning inward and using our mind's eye. Still, what we *think* we know always needs to be tested. Unless our subjective impressions are taken on the road, so to speak, it is impossible to sort out and verify our internal experience.

If the proof of the pudding is in the eating, human relationships are the proof of our understanding of subjective reality. If what we have understood through internal work proves valid in our relationships, we know we're on the right track. The feedback we receive from others helps us expand and deepen our understanding.

Relationships are mirrors which show us how and what we are communicating. If others respond defensively to us, it is likely that we are triggering their defensiveness. Certainly others may have their own reasons for exhibiting defensiveness, yet we can usually modify our behavior to achieve non-defensive communication. We can notice whether we are projecting an attitude toward them, or holding a negative attitude toward ourselves which they're picking up non-verbally. If, for example, someone exhibits a trait I dislike, I am prompted to ask myself if it's a trait I want to overcome within myself. If, on the other hand, someone responds positively toward me, I can assume in the relational dance that I am doing something right.

The fact is a virtual communication highway exists between each of us, constructed of hundreds of non-verbal signals. Even intentions toward others get communicated, whether or not we articulate them. For example, if you regard someone with love, they sense it and respond accordingly. If you feel judgmental about someone, they register your disapproval and mirror it back. Someone we judge harshly, sensing this, will contract. We observe, then, that they look contracted and unattractive. We might wrongly conclude from their unappealing appearance that our negative judgment of them was correct.

A simple way to test the power of intentions is with a domestic dog or cat, if you own one. Approach the animal with the unspoken intention of medicating them, and watch them contract. Approach them with thoughts of dinnertime in mind and see how compliant, receptive and eager they are toward you.

The power of intention is readily apparent, if you but observe. If someone triggers a negative response within you, that person invariably will shrink from your unspoken thoughts. If we switch from negative to positive, if we treat another as though he or she is a precious person, a gem, that person will receive this non-verbal message and often will rise to the occasion. Increased confidence generated from our positive regard will enhance that person's radiance, aliveness and attractiveness. Essentially, we are one thought or intention away from achieving harmony with those with whom we relate. It all depends on what thought you choose.

Fear is reflected through mirroring the same way as negative judgment or positive regard. If we see another person's fear, we may feel a pull, an induction, to feel the same way. We can resist the pull, however, if we identify the fear in someone else. Recognizing their fear for what it is, we can instead reflect back to them courage or confidence. This helps them defuse their fear and keeps us from losing our equanimity.

Similarly, if we are not in integrity, it will be reflected back to us, maybe not immediately, but ultimately it will. Dishonesty contains the seeds of its own undoing. People who are aligned with their true nature will not only have difficulty feeling okay about lying, but they will also easily sense or perceive when someone else is lying. At some level, any of us knows when someone is lying, but we may ignore this if we are caught up in wishful thinking – wanting to believe in something or someone representing some desire we're attached to. Or we might overlook the lie if we are mentally lazy and don't follow up on doubts we may have.

If everyone were able to quiet their minds, tune in to their heart, gut, intuition, and even better, to receive information from Source or from the One Mind, then simple precise truths would become the basis of people's decision-making.

"There are phenomenal capacities in honesty that simply don't exist otherwise. Honesty expands and resonates with other minds and communities, while corrupt minds tend to collapse into themselves. They don't connect, in a larger sense, because they're too self-absorbed and predatory."

~ George LoBuono, *Alien Mind*

Our generosity toward others – our willingness to give the benefit of the doubt or to assume the best of them – comes from our generosity toward ourselves. If we feel badly about ourselves, we may project our negative self-judgment onto others. If we're loving toward ourselves, we can be loved by others. The mirror principle works in the positive and the negative. What we put out is reflected back to us. So we owe it to ourselves to put out positive, or we invite negativity.

It seems like magic happens when we cherish ourselves and postpone our negative judgments toward others until and unless they act badly or unethically. When our attitude toward others is generous, we get back a generous attitude, even when we meet new people. We discover new beauty in others. We feel so enriched by the love surrounding us we wonder why we didn't notice before how much love is available to us.

CHAPTER 12.

THE SOCIAL NECESSITY FOR CREATIVITY AND THE RADICAL SPIRIT

The Necessity for Envisioning a Different World

Intuition and Inner Guidance can be powerfully applied for social change once they're brought into mental focus and given meaning in daily life. They feed the imagination, which draws the blueprints for alternate realities. An individual does not create within a vacuum, however. Every human creation also draws from ideas and information emanating from the social world and the surrounding environment. Creativity is *ultimately a social process*.

The loss of imagination, on the other hand, implies the loss of human freedom. Psychology and psychoanalysts have generally envisioned freedom as freedom from neurosis rather than as freedom to create something new. According to Sigmund Freud, Western civilization demanded the suppression of instinct, which creates conflict and frustration for the individual, resulting in neuroses. The only alternative to neurosis was to channel these drives into less direct modes of expression, such as art, invention or religion, which can be acceptable to society. (Freud 1929) The imagination was not viewed as the motor of creativity, and was not considered essential to social evolution except in a limited way. Freud did not envision a higher stage of social evolution except that brought about through psychoanalysis, helping to relieve people of neurotic misery.

From the vantage point of the present, it is perhaps easier to understand the *necessity* for envisioning a different social order, even if only because we have witnessed the enormous destructiveness of warfare, ecological disaster, economic chaos, the callous profiteering of mega-banks and mega-corporations, for-sale politicians, and extreme forms of personal alienation. Given this, one begins to realize the critical need for expansive and immediate social evolution.

Envisioning a different possible world is also made easier, given the availability of technological and material means for reordering and redistributing social wealth. Information, energy, telecommunications and other common services are all radically decentralized and people have access to these in ways never before possible.

Radical Spirit, Rational Mind

While much creative and constructive activity has been employed to address multiple urgent crises facing us at this time, many people still are walking through life bewildered, numbed, discouraged, without direction. They still are acquiescing to the culture of passive consumption and survivalism. In the end, this is a losing stratagem, for by so doing we are quietly destroying the very foundations of personal, social and environmental sustainability, to say nothing of our own sense of well being. To acquiesce is to invite a slow, certain death.

One can die by a thousand pinpricks, which is today, death by a thousand increments of the power of the corporate state and banking elite. They take their tithing of other peoples' blood and toil daily: consider the time spent in soul-numbing jobs; inflation to support untold trillions spent on endless wars of Empire; health being steadily ruined by food that doesn't nourish, by poisoned air and water. Steadily "the Commons" (the forests, atmosphere, rivers, fisheries or grazing land – once shared, used and enjoyed by all) are being pillaged and privatized. That which once was sacred – higher intelligence and respect for nature – has taken fatal blows or gone into hiding. When it returns, which it inevitably must, it will be in a form more suited to the present time.

It is increasingly clear that the old order, industrial – and now global – corporate capitalism in its present form has outlived its usefulness. The proverbial bloom is long off the rose. The law of diminishing returns is evident in the desperation of the propagandists' lies that are so ludicrous that only the gullible will fail to see the contradictions in their logic. It is evident in the desperation of ad men to come up with ever-more ridiculous reasons for buying junk, stuff and gadgets; in corporate think tanks and lobbying groups who buy politicians and feed them rationales for continuing the market domination of society and the madness of consumerism, the madness of turning all productive resources to what will turn a profit. Consider but one of the many egregious examples: pharmaceutical companies who capitalize on disease rather than on curing it. Drug companies invent medications for entirely preventable cancers, medications which are in themselves often lethal. And now the drug companies are developing a pill to eliminate stress. These profiteers are overlooking two essential and obvious facts: one, stress results from the individual's reaction to the ubiquitous challenges and unworkability of life now confronting them. Secondly, stress can most easily be alleviated by going within, quieting the mind, and finding the peace that dwells there. Unlike drugs, this approach has no deleterious side effects!

The sheer unworkability of our society at this point in history must eventually force people to throw off the now-powerful organization of the World of Things run by corporate and financial elites. Their world cannot long continue, as it is part and parcel of the marketplace, and the marketplace itself is increasingly unable to give people what they need. As citizens of an unworkable world, we are invited, and soon will be compelled, to throw off the world of things, the frozen roles and social hierarchy that has dominated subjective reality – the world of human desires, consciousness and imagination. [See Notes, Chapter 12: "Capital"]

Out of the Matrix: Breakaway Solutions

People aligned with their true nature will easily recognize what is uplifting and instinctively reject what is oppressive and false. This is the starting point for radical creativity, which breaks the shackles of conventionality, uproots the entire problematic structure and re-visions it. This is happening more and more around the world, as the pain and unworkability of the old systems midwifes the new.

Consider, for example, the many "sustainable communities" around the globe which operate off the grid, unplugged from "the Matrix." By creating their own alternative currencies and barter systems, a growing number of communities in the U.S. are just "walking away" from the corrupt financial system, big banks, and their rigged game, however transitional these community programs may be. Scandinavia and Germany have radically transitioned their economies to more sustainable energy systems.

Breakaway solutions will not easily be implemented. Yet, such solutions are necessary if humanity is to survive. Bold creativity is essential now if the decaying order is to be successfully challenged and overcome. Change-oriented groups recognized that humanity stands at the precipice now, the critical point at which we decide whether to save ourselves and the environment, or to perpetuate an obsolete system whose rapaciousness is destroying the global biosphere.

When faced with the unworkability of life as they've known it, in the past, people have turned to religion, some God as they knew It, or to utopian visions. Each of these solutions was seen as separate from daily life. What seems necessary now is to merge spirituality, vision and daily life *as lived in the real world.* Like the phoenix rising, we must create a new society out of the ashes.

We are encouraged to take a new approach, to recognize that the spiritual essence of every individual and sentient being is joined, and that what harms one, harms us all. We are invited now to recognize and reverse acts that are destroying our planetary biosphere. As in the past, with cultures that honored Nature, we must again learn from and begin to work with Nature, fully understanding that we too are an integral part of Nature.

Chapter 13.

The Activation of the Human Spirit for Social Liberation

Herbert Marcuse wrote extensively about how, in our society, nearly every human activity and its products are sold into the service of the dominant culture, leaving the individual cut off from his creations. Thus, at best, the individual must exist as a contemplative or frenetic being; at worst, as an automaton, neurotic, or psychotic. In the contemplative, psychic life rages unseen beneath the calm surface; in the frenetic person, life simply rages, uncontrolled (witness the 'impulsive character' or the psychopath). In both cases, he writes, the instinctual energies, rationality and imagination strive toward autonomy, albeit either in a 'fictitious world' of fantasy, or through violent destruction of the social order. (Marcuse 1977)

The spark of individual creativity is the *sine qua non* of social change. At the societal level change only happens through the collective efforts of individuals who take their desires seriously, and from this point formulate visions of a new society.

Authentic common life arises not through reflection; rather it comes about from the need and egoism of individuals, that is, immediately from the activation of their very existence. ...So long as man does not recognize himself as man and does not organize the world humanly, this common life appears in the form of alienation, because its subject, man, is a being alienated from itself.

~ Karl Marx

Creativity comes when one taps into the core of one's being. Once that happens, the illusions fall away. The world is seen for what it is. Without going as far as retreating into communion with no one but God, as a hermit or solitary monk – increasingly difficult in a densely populated world – one must face the Beast and stare it down.

"Imagination nourishes utopianism.
Far from leading to a totalitarian society,
imagination threatens it."

~Yevgeny Zamyatin

Imagination has been the missing ingredient in past social movements, revolutions and utopian communities. They usually failed because they were premised on closed non-dynamic systems and ideologies, which enabled the growth of new power elites and bureaucracies. These in turn were able to wrest away from working people the control over their own lives and the products of their labor.

Guggenheim Fellow and history professor at UCLA, Dr. Russell Jacoby, offers a spectrum of reasons for the demise of utopian envisioning, including the dwindling force of the modern imagination:

Is it possible that imagination – the source of utopian speculation – has lost its vigor? That a relentless barrage of prefabricated "images" from movies and advertising has shackled its linguistic and factual offering, "imagination"? Has imagination become unimaginative – or rather practical and realistic? The topic is difficult to circumscribe and my concerns resist proof… [my students] come up with laudable ideas – universal health care with choice of doctors; free higher education; clean parks; ecological vehicles – but very little that is out of the ordinary. Their boldest dreams could be realized by a comprehensive welfare state.… A world without utopian longings is forlorn. For society as well as for the individual, it means to journey without a compass. (Jacoby 2007)

The Old System Cannot be Repaired

"Things fall apart; the center cannot hold;
Mere anarchy is loosed upon the world,
The blood-dimmed tide is loosed, and everywhere
The ceremony of innocence is drowned;
The best lack all conviction, while the worst
Are full of passionate intensity."

"The Second Coming"
~ William Butler Yeats

Civilization as we have known it on Planet Earth is being upended. It is rent through with divisions and cracks that cannot be patched.

Because the systems of old are completely interdependent, whatever repair is made to part of the system cannot hold. If only one part is repaired, it will inevitably succumb to the disorder of the rest of the system.

Each of us is subject to the symptoms of decay and decline, except insofar we can train ourselves through integrative understanding to see the whole while standing outside it. Buddhists refer to this as "detachment." Our actions, however, must be within the context of the environment. The actions a need to be a positive influence, not coming from a cynical desire just to get by, get rich, or get the spoils. If we act from a motive other than creating good, our integrity is compromised and our spiritual vessel is cracked. Without integrity, we are prevented from accessing higher understanding and fulfilling our evolutionary potential. Furthermore, if the voice of conscience is repeatedly ignored, it may become extinguished altogether. Then one has stepped over the line to the "dark side," perhaps irretrievably.

A great shift in human awareness is now taking place. Regrettably, not all humans will be able to embrace the new levels of understanding. Those unable to evolve will fare badly. They will remain mired in old ways of being. Conversely, those able to comprehend the new emerging patterns will fulfill their human potential to greater or lesser degrees.

According to Guidance I received on this matter, individuals aligned with their inner integrity will advance to the next level of evolutionary progress. Unaligned persons, through exposure to those who are aligned may, however, be inducted into a greater degree of alignment themselves.

Further, according to my Guidance, the unaligned persons will not complete the transition to the next evolutionary level until and unless their understanding is enhanced commensurately. This will happen only if these individuals solemnly decide to undertake the introspective self-evaluation required to identify the shortcomings in their behavior. Further, they must improve their behavior and their treatment of others. Anyone who sincerely desires to become more perfected shall find offered to them, by the Creator, any assistance required.

The immensity of the task ahead can seem overwhelming. An enormous gap exists between what our society is equipped to do and what needs to be done. In the past quarter century society has experienced an exponential increase in the number of people who are homeless, unemployed and sick. The rate of illiteracy is staggering. Global population is expected to reach between 7.5 and 10.5 billion by the year 2050. (Wikipedia/World population) We're consuming resources and polluting our planet at an unprecedented and unsustainable rate. How can the human race survive? Objectively speaking, it looks hopeless.

Subjectively, what is needed is a radically creative spirit that fires the individual with vision and imagination to implement new beginnings, that refuses complacency and refuses old partial solutions doomed to fail in the long, if not the short term.

Clear analysis is also required and reveals the increasingly obvious truth: capital is the ultimate whore, trading blood and souls anywhere, anytime. It will continue to satisfy its voracious appetites only when nothing remains to be profitably exploited. It has become a god of lies. Unbridled capitalism is the horse that has overthrown its rider.

What was once a useful system for aggregating capital, necessary to build more efficient methods of production, has become self-cannibalizing. The system is unstable. Its inherent contradictions now are finally emerging to force its undoing. It is time to bridle the beast, to use capital for new endeavors that make the leap in development to more integrated systems that work with nature, and for humans.

As Russell Jacoby writes, in the past, revolutionary movements have been fueled by the promise of a better world. Insofar as these movements have been defined merely in terms of opposition to the outmoded previous social order, the new social orders contained the fatal flaw of merely being the antithesis – the upside-down reflection, too much a reverse-mirror of what went before. Thesis and antithesis resolves themselves in synthesis, but what resolved the contradictions in the first half of the twentieth century were National Socialism and Bolshevik Communism. (Jacoby 2007)

What is needed now is a transcendent society, one that supersedes the old, one that does not fall into the reverse-mirroring antithesis. On the practical level, this would more closely resemble the mixed economies of the Scandinavian countries. It would incorporate the best of the market economy, rewarding innovation, efficiency, and production of goods that people really need. It would require that speculation be taxed, that anti-trust laws be enforced, and that commercial banks be regulated as they were under the Glass-Steagall Act.* Currently regressive tax rates could be reformed to be closer to what they were in the prosperous 1950's and '60's, when the highest income tax bracket was 91%, not 35 or 39.

This new kind of society would compel the federal government to support such projects as the rebuilding of infrastructure and the educational system; it would subsidize green energy technologies rather than environmentally destructive energy sources like coal, oil and nuclear. The government would be charged with protection of the environment and the commons, and would provide a more rational form of social safety net. Conservation and respect for Nature, not taking more from Nature than is replaced, would be essential. Emphasis would be placed on the values of non-material qualities of life, and consumerism would be demoted.

Once dangers are clearly seen, good people get motivated and involved. In fact, transformation is already happening, here and there, some piecemeal, some more systematic and comprehensive. But such transformations must be driven by a critical mass of citizens connected locally as well as globally. The rapid growth of online "social networking" attests to the great longing and *desire* people have for connection. And yet, face-to-face encounters are where the real payoff lies. Consider, for example, the "Occupy movement," launched in the U.S. in Fall 2011. Here people united to confront political and financial injustice. Connections formed during such

---

*Also known as the Banking Act of 1933, this Act prohibited bank holding companies from owning other financial companies. The repeal of one of its provisions in 1999 effectively removed the separation between investment banking which issued securities and commercial banks which accepted deposits. This opened the door once again to uncontrolled speculation on the part of commercial banks. The repeal enabled commercial lenders such as Citigroup (which in 1999 was the largest U.S. bank by assets), to underwrite and trade instruments such as mortgage-backed securities and collateralized debt obligations and establish so-called structured investment vehicles, or SIVs, that bought those securities. (Wikipedia, "Glass-Steagall Act")

events can endure and lead to ongoing social creativity and problem-solving. Although this movement is no longer organized as such, the ideas it put forth signaled the reawakening of the radically creative social spirit on a broad scale.

Radical Spirit and Vision

From radical spirit comes radically honest perception, plus a clear understanding of what will work. From these, right action follows. In the process, the blinders of pseudo-happiness are removed.

Those who accept that life is necessarily filled with unhappiness – a bowl of pits rather than cherries – have not allowed themselves to dream, or to honor what they secretly know to be true and what they truly want out of life. They may even achieve power, wealth, and prestige, but still be haunted by a restless dissatisfaction and feeling of emptiness. The wealthy individual who thinks he or she can buy his way out of discomfort, eventually confronts profound isolation, or the resentment and hatred of those on whose backs he has stepped to gain his wealth. Wealthy people may circumvent the globe in search of security, only to discover they can't get their money out of their foreign investments and there is no place to escape the world's problems. Those who run from themselves, in effect, meet themselves coming and going.

Late in this Age of Industrialization, we are taunted and challenged by extremes. We have seen the steady concentration of wealth in the hands of the few, extreme weather patterns and changes in climate, extreme polarities in ideologies and systems of moral beliefs, extreme alienation Nature, to the point of working against

Nature herself. This has been, unfortunately, the necessary playing out of collective humanity's best understandings of our present cycle or age.

The relentless timeline of history has brought us to the inevitable, and for the most part, predictable outcome of extremes standing in unambiguous contrast. In hindsight, the patterns have become clear. In the present, the choices become somewhat clear. We have reached a crossroad: either we clutch tightly onto a world that is dying, or we side with the evolutionary path.

We are really facing a species crisis. Those who see themselves as part of a living whole, who tap their innermost resources of creativity and live cooperatively as strong individuals, will continue to evolve and survive.

Homo Spiritualis

This crossroad brings us to new awareness and new ways of being. Christopher Bache describes the great transition our species must make. In his words, we must become *homo spiritualis:*

> If the crisis of sustainability does bring about the ego-death of our species, what will have died, I think, is primarily our sense of being disconnected from each other and from everything around us. As the psychological debris of our difficult past is cleared away, we will begin to experience more clearly the web that weaves all life into a single fabric. … The adventure is now inherently collective. The age of the hero is yielding to the age of the heroic community. If the community does not become heroically realized, no individual heroes will survive to chase dragons.

As the inherent wholeness of existence becomes a living experience for more and more persons, individuals will find themselves empowered by new orders of creativity that could not have been anticipated as long as we were trapped within the narrow confines of an atomistic, self-referential mode of consciousness. As the encompassing fields of mind become stronger, synergy and synchronicity will increase. The Sacred Mind will spring alive inside the human family in ways that seem impossible from our current fragmented condition. However difficult the journey, who could not feel uplifted by the privilege of being part of such an undertaking? The pain of this labor should not be feared but used creatively. We are building a new world for our grandchildren, indeed, a new species – *Homo spiritualis*. (Bache 2000)

Socrates once said, "The unexamined life is not worth living." Through disciplined self-inquiry, one inevitably gets to what is truly meaningful. The human psyche is purposive. Aligning with one's purpose can be rewarded with inspiration. Hail its arrival, for inspiration, vision and quality of life are integral components of our next evolutionary phase. These components translate to people claiming their power.

As humans we have the inherent ability to shape our experience, and our evolutionary path. At this juncture, evolution is the only viable path. We must attain higher intelligence and understanding to support our environment and to revive and restore the now-fading flower that is human civilization.

CHAPTER 14.

DESIGNING A FUTURE IN HARMONY WITH NATURE

I have always had a deep love for nature and an instinctual sense that its wisdom is fathomless and sacred. When, in the late 1960's, I returned to the West coast after spending two years in Massachusetts where my then-husband was studying for his PhD, I intuitively felt that the Pacific Ocean was in grave trouble. I could sense the polluted quality of the water just from being near it. This grieved me deeply. I was in no position to do anything about this or to be an environmentalist for a number of ensuing years. But later, in Fairfax, after I quit my psychotherapy practice, I set about trying to do environmental work. My experiences in the garden taught me much about the subtle connections among all living things. So deep was my reverence for nature and my horror at the disrespect being heaped upon her that I spent two years working at environmental projects. These included promoting and doing vermiculture for soil remediation and recycling, selling architectural building products made from recycled materials, and learning about full-cost accounting, whereby the costs of natural resources, resource extraction, pollution remediation and recycling are included in the cost of producing goods. Unfortunately, none of these endeavors could pay my bills, and so I went on to other occupations, but my deep respect for Nature endures. Now I do what I can to help educate others about Nature and ecological systems.

Few assaults on Mother Nature have alarmed me more than modern-day developments in the genetic modification of the DNA of plant, animal and human life. In nature, many different elements at the most basic level are balanced in a complex equation designed to ensure the unfolding of a higher evolutionary schema. When humans interfere with the design of nature, irreparable damage is done to the fundamental systems supporting all of life.

The Folly of Bio-Engineering

Scientists in the field of bioengineering believe they can improve on the design of nature. They are, in fact, working against nature. They are taking a piecemeal approach, with little or no apparent understanding of the greater whole, the intricately interwoven and interdependent web of life. Changing the genetic code of a plant or animal can have consequences far beyond the imaginations and understanding of most scientists, and certainly beyond their official levels of responsibility. As well, changing the genetics in the human genome is a reckless endeavor, pure and simple. These bio-engineers have inadequate understanding of the human body taken as a whole – a body wherein every cell has intelligence and all are linked in a subtle network of information connectivity throughout the human body. Changing the underlying pattern changes all.

It seems pure hubris to believe one can improve upon the design embedded in the code of human DNA. That design is calculated precisely to integrate with the evolutionary process embedded/encoded in the DNA of the entire natural world, including the human species.

Dr. Mae-Wan Ho, chief scientist of the Institute of Science in Society in the UK, warns that further indulgence in GMOs (genetically modified organisms) will severely damage our chances of surviving the food crisis and global climate change. Organic agriculture and localized food systems are the way forward, she says. Furthermore, genetic modification is based on an obsolete theory and hence is ineffective and dangerous:

> The best thing about the human genome project is to finally explode the myth of genetic determinism, revealing the layers of molecular complexity that transmit, interpret and rewrite the genetic texts. These processes are precisely orchestrated and finely tuned by the organism as a whole, in a highly coordinated molecular 'dance of life' that's necessary for survival.
>
> In contrast, genetic engineering in the laboratory is crude, imprecise and invasive. The rogue genes inserted into a genome to make a GMO could land anywhere – typically in a rearranged or defective form, scrambling and mutating the host genome – and have the tendency to move or rearrange further once inserted, basically because *they do not know the dance of life*. [italics author's] That's

ultimately why genetic modification doesn't work and is also dangerous. (Ho 2006) [See Notes: "GMO Foods" for more]

Despite Nature's mounting protests – storms, floods, droughts, and other environmental catastrophes – the human race *is* des-tined to continueits evolutionary journey. Once humanity gains sufficient understanding of utter complexity of reality obsolete ideas are overturned and the next evolutionary step reveals itself. Storms, floods, droughts, and other environmental catastrophes notwithstanding, the human race is destined to continue its evo-lutionary journey. The architecture of change supersedes individuals' determination to maintain their independence from the essentially interdependent whole. Nature will win in the long run, as will the interconnected evolutionary thrust of all living beings, the human species included.

In 2004, computer models designed to predict the sustainability of global society gave us fifteen years at that year's rate of consuming natural resources and polluting the environment. (Meadows and Randers 2004) These models correlate interactions of capital inputs, rates of using resources, topsoil depletion, pollution and population growth. But the 2004 model failed to include such variables as face us now – climate change, the spread of disease, and political instabilities. Certainly these factors also contribute to our spiral of decline.

Yet still many people hold the prevailing "I'll get mine" mentality. Of what value is personal wealth when our ecosystem has but ten years to live? If our ecosystem dies, the strongest fortress won't hold enough oxygen to breathe, clean water to drink or living soil to grow food.

Unpredictable as resource usage and political realities are, certain facts are quite clear. A four-degree increase in global warming could so alter weather patterns that agriculture would be severely affected. Already temperature changes are adversely affecting agriculture in many regions. (Given the need for proper soil conditions and adequate water, it is impractical at best to assume we can relocate crops to areas where the weather may be more suitable.)

Melting polar ice caps are causing a rise in sea level. Low-lying island nations are being inundated. In many coastal areas, salt water is infiltrating water tables and flooding wetlands and marshes where fish breed. And, when the polar ice melt cools the upper loop of the Atlantic conveyor belt – the current that brings warm water north from the tropics, we could well experience *abrupt* climate change – a sudden onset of the next ice age.

Pollution has a cumulative effect on health, so sickness is destined to increase exponentially. In fact, it has happened already. In the 1940s, one out of twelve humans in the United States were destined to suffer from cancer. Now it is one out of two. Polluted soil produces nutrient-poor food, which contributes to malnutrition and lowered disease resistance. Unless we maintain excellent health, each of us is subject to air- and water-borne pathogens, which further compromise our health.

Life energy demands to be used. If we don't employ it positively, it will be used destructively. At this time, entire segments of our global society are immersed in chaos. Unchanneled energy is being expressed destructively wherever new forms for its constructive use have not been created. The most glaring example is fanatic fundamentalism in the Middle East, expressed by disenfranchised people with nothing to lose. In the US and Latin America, violent drug gangs are the last resort of people with no education, no skills, no jobs, in short, nothing left to lose.

On the flip side of the coin, necessity is forcing those who are able, to evolve. Visions of new ways of organizing society are emerging where the old ways no longer work. Creativity is arising in response to necessity. Designs are being created, blueprints drawn, and technologies developed. The following chapters detail many of these efforts. Learning is accelerating, thanks to the Internet. If wars don't destroy all the wealth accumulated by global society, there is enough now to make whatever we need, enough to construct essential foundations upon which to build our future, and enough to improve our lives continuously, globally.

Sustainable communities and societies are those that acknowl-edge our interdependence. They practice respect and positive regard for all of life. Sustainable economic systems return to the earth as much as they take out. We must now utilize only those materials that can be recycled into new products or returned to the earth to support nature's cycles of decomposition and regeneration.

Current and future competition for scarce natural resources will, it is hoped, create increasing pressure to use renewable natural resources, to harvest sustainably, to stop wasting resources and to restore damaged ecosystems. If we hold that vision and act upon it, our global society just may earn itself a future!

CHAPTER 15.

STEPS TO CREATING A NEW SOCIETY

Positive regard is contagious and can spread anywhere.
The love we give is given to the next person and the next.
Love is radioactive.

The art of living is the art of loving. We could shape our entire lives around efforts to be loving. Consider the transformation that might result. Board members of a corporation could decide their company should do the most loving thing it is capable of doing, which would be to provide something of true value to its customers and the planet, according to that company's capabilities. What's needed is valued, and, in an ideal society, value translates directly into payment for services or goods. Any company that offers true value, does, in fact, see the value of their stock soar.

The Banking System

Regrettably, this vision will never be realized on a wide scale unless and until revolutionary changes are made to our banking system and primarily unregulated monopoly capitalism – now global corporate capitalism. The current banking system, the United States' central bank, the Federal Reserve System, formed in 1913, is actually a banking cartel. It is not a government institution, as implied by its name, but a system of privately owned banks authorized by the Congress – a hybrid system. Neither the President nor anyone else in the executive or legislative branch of government is required to ratify the Fed's decisions. While the Fed is subject to congressional oversight, in reality, Congress exercises this authority very little, because Congress depends on the Federal Reserve as the lender of last resort.

The Federal Reserve controls the money supply in the United States through manipulating interest rates and printing money to cover deficit spending by the government. Through fractional reserve banking, banks are allowed to lend beyond what they have in reserves. If, for instance, a bank receives $10 from a depositor, the bank can lend all but a fraction of it. That fraction is kept in "reserve." Whoever borrows that $9 is allowed to lend all but a fraction of that. And on it goes. In the 1970's a ratio of 3:1 was considered normal; one third of a deposit was kept in the bank as a "reserve" of capital, and the remainder could be loaned to others at interest. This formula has changed in a radical and alarming way. The Federal Reserve itself is currently leveraged at 54:1 of liabilities to capital versus 24:1 in September 2007. (Board of Governors of the Federal Reserve System 2011)

If a bank makes a bad loan, say, a loan to a borrower who is unable to pay the interest and thus forfeits his assets (a home, for example), the bank is stuck with illiquidity. Should this happen *en masse*, as it has, the banks that made these bad loans are in trouble. If the Government "bails out" these banks, the taxpayer becomes the fall guy, assuming responsibility for banks that made the bad loans in the first place. What has happened is that there has been no incentive for banks to be careful to avoid bad loans, because they are assured that the Government will bail them out. Instead, banks' shareholders, senior management, and unsecured bondholders are incentivized to make risky loans and other actions, knowing that the Federal Reserve will bail them out with emergency loans, ultra-low interest rates, and by valuing the loans at "mark-to-myth," as opposed to "mark-to-market" value.

In 2008, the larger U.S. banks that made bad loans were not allowed to fail. Period. The reason was simple: the beneficiaries of the loans – those banks collecting interest on the faulty loans – are interlocked with the Federal Reserve system and are part of the cartel, doing what cartels always do, which is protect their interest. And in order to do this, the Fed continues to print money, thereby inflating the money supply, which lowers the purchasing power of the "federal reserve note" – our paper currency. Thus they are killing the golden goose – the working person who borrows money from the banks and has to pay interest on the loan.

There are many schools of thought about how to reform the banking system. I would agree with those who say that reform would need to include breaking up the monopolies, the so-called "Too Big to Fail" financial companies, especially JP Morgan, Bank of America, Citibank, Morgan Stanley and Goldman Sachs. If limits are placed on the amount of assets one bank or bank holding company can control, it cannot have, in effect, monopoly power over smaller banks. A further proposal involves prohibiting

FDIC-insured banks from engaging in proprietary trading, investment banking, or trading over-the-counter derivatives.

To return to a sound money system, some financial analysts insist that the dollar must be backed by something that retains its value, such as precious metals. This would prevent unlimited inflation of the money supply, uncontrolled government spending, plus the increasing flight of capital to other countries. While the concept is valid, only an expanding money supply can keep up with growth in population and productivity, so the gold standard as such is impractical.

An increasingly popular concept holds that "fiat" money, *per se,* is a bad thing. But "fiat" simply means "Let it be done," in other words, fiat money is worth only what people agree it is worth. Agreements are based on trust. If one party to an agreement breaks trust with the other party, the agreement about the value of that particular currency or medium of exchange breaks down. As John Medlin, a Santa Monica-based investment manager, explains,

> All money is and always has been 'fiat,' let it be done. Governments must specify the system of money to be used in its country. The crucial issue is how it is to be 'valued.' It can be done by government edict; however, this edict must have some reality with regards to its value in the marketplace, else a currency black market develops. Money will always find its level, whether gold, silver, Federal Reserve Notes, Bolivars, etc.

In the opinion of Medlin (shared by a number of economists),

"What we are most likely to have in the next three to six years is a new global currency used by banks for their reserves only and not available to the public. This reserve currency will likely be based on the various major currencies and also major commodities – gold and oil."

This may be a good solution for the "haves" – the owners of banks and large corporations who seek ease of trade globally. But it does nothing to address or relieve the increasing impoverishment of working-class people.

Monopolies

A more fundamental problem than banking system reform, however, and one which economists rarely address, is the inevitable tendency in unregulated capitalism for monopolies to be formed. And now we have global monopoly-capitalism. Monopolies, by definition, have no competition, and are therefore free to set whatever prices they choose.

Corporate wealth is such that corporations now unabashedly buy legislators and advance their own presidential candidates. The only thing that can put a rein on their ruthless and relentless global pursuit of profit without regard for social or environmental well being is a widespread grassroots movement, comprised of ordinary people organized to take back what is theirs – the wealth that they themselves have created.

Exactly how this can be accomplished remains to be seen. Globalization (including NAFTA) has opened up such a vast new pool of labor that any U.S. jobs that can profitably be off-shored will in all likelihood continue to be off-shored or done in other countries. In addition, many of the jobs that remain in the U.S. are being filled by foreigners. [See Notes, Chapter 15, "Offshoring."]

Beyond Capitalism and Socialism

The inevitable and foreseeable current crisis of capitalism must be addressed. If it is not addressed rationally, with restructured economic systems, then it will be addressed with violence.

Nordic Societies – part of the way there

Nordic societies have achieved much more equitable and sustainable economic systems that combine the best of capitalism with the best of socialism. These societies acknowledge the need for both markets and central planning, combining positive elements of socialism and capitalism, as well as caring for people and nature. Sweden has effectively demonstrated that sustainability policies and programs can contribute to a nation's prosperity. This country proves that responsible and sustainable growth can co-exist to the benefit of all. (*Sydney Morning Herald 2007;* New European Economy 2007)

The Writing is on the Wall

Many believe the economic crisis in the U.S. has resulted from speculation, printing ever more money to keep the game going, and government bailouts preserving insolvent banks and companies. In fact, the problem goes much deeper than that, and so must the solutions.

We saw the obvious evidence of the problems inherent in capitalism re-emerging in the 1970's when real wages stopped rising (despite workers' productivity consistently increasing). This was due largely to US capitalists investing in off-shore production and employment while simultaneously replacing millions of employees in the US with computers and low-paid non-unionized workers. Women's liberation invited millions of US women to seek paid employment. Given that there was no longer a shortage of labor, employers were able to keep wages frozen. (Wolff 2011)

Certainly opportunities exist for unemployed workers to re-train themselves, to learn new marketable skills. However, the sheer number of unemployed and underemployed people – according to the Bureau of Labor Statistics, January 2016, one in ten Americans – is a fact which cannot be ignored. The sheer force of numbers demands radical solutions. The "Occupy Wall Street" movement, launched in October 2011 and quickly spreading world-wide, stood as a visible reaction to the dire circumstances faced by unemployed college graduates and people of all ages whose wealth has been decimated by the "Great Recession." People were beginning to see the writing on the wall: the Federal Government was, and is, willing to push the country to the brink and beyond by inflating the money supply, increasing the national debt, and delaying the day of reckoning, which day is perilously close.

During the election cycle of 2016, there has been an unforeseen upsurge of enthusiasm and support for Senator Bernie Sanders, running as a socialist, for the President of the United States. Not since the anti-communism sentiment of the McCarthy Era of the 1950's has socialism been a part of the national dialogue. That it is now being debated nationally as an alternative to present-day capitalism is in itself a sign that working people are extremely upset about the current economic system. It may perhaps also be a sign that the ideas voiced by the Occupy Movement have taken root in the broader public.

The surge of support for socialist Bernie Sanders has been fueled in large part by the youth vote. This should not be too surprising, as millennials (as well as with middle-aged workers), have been hit by a number of harsh economic factors: wage stagnation (decades-long); followed by wage decline during the Great Recession; high unemployment following the financial crash; not to mention much higher health care costs.

The New Republic magazine, Feb. 10, 2016, reported that while unemployment has dropped to 4.9 percent overall, it is at 16 percent for those between the ages of 16 and 19, and 8.2 percent for 20-to-24-year-olds....Young people today are also much less likely to have employer-sponsored health care than in the past.

Millennials are saddled with debt, their economic opportunities are far more limited than that of any recent generation, and often they are working three jobs and paying for the Social Security benefits of current and soon to be retirees.)

The increasing inability of employed workers to make a living wage adds to the dry tinder that might one day soon ignite. According Richard D. Wolff, Professor of Economics Emeritus at University of Massachusetts, Amherst and currently Visiting Professor at New School University in New York City,

... real wages stagnated in the US since the 1970s. Over the same period, workers' productivity – the quantities of goods and services they produced for their employers to sell – rose consistently. Real hourly output per worker rose 45 per cent since 1990, while total compensation per

worker (wages and salaries *plus all benefits)* rose 25 per cent. The difference between the two numbers – between what employers get from their workers and what they pay for their workers – accrues as rising business net revenues. Out of those revenues, employers pay dividends to shareholders, salaries and bonuses to top managers, and funds to grow the businesses. The last several decades of flat wages and rising productivity explain the growing distance separating the rich from the middle and the poor.

Workers, in short, failed to achieve rising incomes that matched their rising productivity. They were, in short, increasingly exploited. Their rising productivity fueled insteadtheexplodinggainsfortopmanagersandshareholders. Borrowing unprecedented sums only postponed facing up to what was happening while adding the burdens of rising debt to those of rising exploitation. (Wolff 2009)

Not only are wages less, relative to the time, skills and effort put into creating a product or service, but, because of an inflated money supply from deficit financing, that wage has less purchasing power. This constitutes an anomaly of the tallest order, for according to statistics documenting productivity, the average worker in the United States, Europe and Japan, needs to work a mere eleven hours per week to produce as much as a person working forty hours in 1950! If productivity – and not corporate greed – were the measure, a worker should maintain the same standard of living as a 1950 worker in only eleven hours per week.

The elites have long envisioned and planned for a neo-feudal society. Economist Michael Hudson describes their scheme aptly:

> Instead of enjoying what the Progressive Era anticipated – an evolution into socialism, with government providing basic infrastructure and other needs on a subsidized basis – we are seeing a lapse back into neo-feudalism. The difference, of course, is that this time around society is not controlled by military grabbers of the land. Finance today achieves what military force did in times past. Instead of being tied to the land as under feudalism, families today may live wherever they want – as long as they take on a lifetime of debt to pay the mortgage on whatever home they buy.
>
> And instead of society paying land rent and tribute to conquerors, we pay the bankers. Just as access to the land was a precondition for families to feed themselves under feudalism, one needs access to credit, to water, medical care, pensions or Social Security and other basic needs today – and must pay interest, fees and monopoly rent to the neo-feudal oligarchy that is now making its deft move from the United States to Ireland and Greece." (Hudson 2011)

Hudson proposes as an alternative a small 's' socialism that relegates central government to providing basic infrastructure – the kinds of investments that are simply not practical to make at a regional level. For example, railroads and highways need to be standardized.

The modern vision must incorporate the right to fair pay, clean air, water, and food, as well as to educational opportunities and affordable health care. But none of these basic rights can be preserved unless it is understood that the role of government is to ensure these basic rights.

Investment in education, health, infrastructure, green-tech, and sustainability for the environment make sense economically and are in fact crucial to the survival of the human race. Government can put policies in place to support these kinds of investments.

The Rubicon has been crossed, and there is no turning back. The national debt cannot be paid. The economic strength of the US cannot be restored without strong measures. Our country will only emerge out of this confluence of crises by formulating and instituting new forms and a new understanding of what the next steps in our evolution as a society must be.

The world population stands now at 7 billion people. Sooner rather than later, resource scarcities will force human society to adopt a sustainable model, in effect a closed-loop, 'steady state' economy premised on nearly 100 percent recycling of materials and 100 percent renewable energy. This new economy will maximize well-being – instead of wealth in the hands of the few. Growth will be encouraged to steadily improve the quality of life, not to steadily increase the quantity of goods consumed. (Jones 2008)

Let me stand at your verge
Chasm, and not be dismayed!

Where irrepressible greed has
Trampled down every inch of
Earth from equator to pole and
Shamelessly wielded relentless
Glare and mastery over
Every nook of the world,

Where in the smothering cells of
Hideous houses, madness has
Just found what will poison
All horizons tomorrow:
Even shepherds in yurts,
Even nomads in wastes.

There in the sorest of trials
Powers below pondered gravely,
Gracious celestials gave their
Ultimate secret: the altered
Laws over matter and founded
Space – a new space in the old.

~ Stefan George, *Secret Germany*

CHAPTER 16.

SO MUCH WORK TO BE DONE –
THE RIGHT WORK

The supreme irony of this age is that there is near-record unemployment while there is so much work to be done – right work – work that adds value to society and improves the quality of our lives. Workers cooperatives are part of the solution. Local organic farms and community-supported agricultural cooperatives are part of the solution. "Green jobs" rebuilding our infrastructure are a part of the solution. And grassroots organizations, linked through growing networks, are a part of the solution….

Living Simply, with All We Really Need

Some argue we should make do with less. This is a program that would likely please the elites, as long as they were not the ones making do with less. Nonetheless, there are ways in which having less makes sense, both in lowering expenses, and in terms of defining what happiness is. The oft-repeated saying goes, wealth alone does not buy happiness. But what does this really mean?

A report released by the OECD (Organization for Economic and Co-operation and Development) in October 2011, helps supply an answer. In an effort to devise new measures for assessing well-being that go beyond Gross Domestic Product, the OECD assessed eleven specific aspects of life – from income, jobs and housing to health, education and the environment. Questions centered around job satisfaction, the status of one's health; the amount of time spent each day with one's children; whether friends are there when you need them; whether you can trust your neighbors; and your overall satisfaction with your life.

The report drew a comprehensive picture of what makes up people's lives in forty countries worldwide. The United States ranked number nineteen, that is, nineteen countries down from the top-ranking Denmark. In concluding, the report said that while income is a prime contributor, other factors matter even more. Well-being is intrinsically linked to good health, a clean environment, a strong sense of community and civic engagement, a home in good shape and a safe neighborhood. (OECD 2011)

Internationally recognized social visionary, Duane Elgin popularized simplified living in his *Voluntary Simplicity,* a book published in 1981. In 2007, in an article entitled, "A Garden of Simplicity Is Growing in the World," Elgin states that, according to surveys, at least ten percent, or more than 20 million, of the adult population of the United States are consciously exploring various expressions of simplicity of living.... And this before the financial crisis of 2008.

Elgin writes,

If we are to create … an 'evolutionary bounce' or leap forward, it will surely include a collective shift toward simpler, more sustainable and satisfying ways of living. Simplicity is not an alternative lifestyle for a marginal few; it is a creative choice for the mainstream majority, particularly in developed nations…. Even with major technological innovations in energy and transportation, dramatic changes will be required in our overall patterns of living and consuming if we are to maintain the integrity of the Earth as a living system. The coming era of constraint can bring focus and energy to crafting lives of elegant and creative simplicity.

Although the ecological pushes toward simpler ways of living are strong, the pulls toward this way of life seem equally compelling. In reality, most people are not choosing to live more simply from a feeling of sacrifice; rather, they are seeking deeper sources of satisfaction than are being offered by a high stress, consumption-obsessed world….[People] are also … moving into a life that is, though materially more modest, rich with family, friends, community, creative work in the world, and a soulful connection with the universe." (Elgin 2007)

Advocating for human-scale community, Elgin concludes,

If given the choice, millions of people would choose new forms of community that support simpler, more sustainable ways of living…. A new architecture of life is needed; one that integrates the physical as well as social and cultural/

spiritual dimensions of our lives. Taking a lesson from humanity's past, it is important to look at the in-between scale of living – that of a small village consisting of a few hundred people or less. Great opportunity exists for organizing into clusters of small ecovillages that are nested within a larger urban area. (Elgin 2007)

At this writing, one online directory alone lists 450 ecovillages worldwide. While representing but a small portion of the population, this shows that people are breaking from consumerism in favor of living sustainably in community.

Mondragon Cooperative Movement

Small-scale communities and villages need not be limited to whatever cottage industries and local farms can produce. With cooperative organization, many possibilities exist for producing locally and selling or trading on a broader scale. An inspiring example is the Mondragon Cooperative Movement.

The Mondragon Corporation is a federation of worker cooperatives based in the Basque region of Spain. Founded in the town of Mondragón in 1956, its origin is linked to the activity of a modest technical college and a small workshop producing paraffin heaters. Currently it is the largest business group in the Basque Country and the tenth largest in Spain. At the end of 2014 it was providing employment for 74,117 people working in 289 companies in four areas of activity: Finance, Industry, Retail and Knowledge. As of 2014, which year marked the end of a recession, 103 of these companies were co-operatives. The Mondragon cooperatives operate in accordance with a business model based on people and the sovereignty of labor, which has made it possible to develop highly participative companies rooted in solidarity, with a strong social dimension but without neglecting business excellence. The Cooperatives are owned by their worker-members and power is based on the principle of one person, one vote.... In 2008, The Mondragon Corporation provided 3.6 % of the Basque Autonomous Community's total GDP and 6.6% of its Industrial GDP. (en.wikipedia.org; www.mondragon-corporation.com/eng/; www.mondragon-corporation.com/eng/about-us/economic-and-financial-indicators/annual-report/)

Economies at the scale of the village, county or region are not the total solution, but they are certainly a part. Simplifying one's life in order to have time to participate in political life is part of the solution. But in our world of international economies, transnational bureaucracies and multinational capitalism, crowned by financial and corporate power, what is left of democracy?

In the Corporatist State, the role of government has been re-defined not as a protector of the well-being of its citizenry, but as an entity to manage "democracy." The State prioritizes the economy's need for political stability, the government's need for a governable citizenry, and the military's need for "rapid response."

Our Sociopathic Culture

Our government is run now by and for the corporations and financial institutions. Its pro-corporate, anti-democratic culture has become increasingly obvious. As political philosopher and professor emeritus Sheldon Wolin writes,

> In its structure, ideology, and human relationships capitalism was [now in late-capitalism] producing human beings unfitted for democratic citizenship: self-interested, exploitive, competitive, striving for inequalities, fearful of downward mobility. One's neighbor was either a rival or a useful object. As the world of capital became steadily more enveloping and the claims of the political more anachronistic, capital became the standard of the "real," the "true world." By that measure democracy – as the carrier of the common good whose promotion required a strong element of egalitarianism, cooperation, and disinterestedness – appeared as untrue, falsified by reality. (Wolin 2004)

Hence, we have a culture that champions a form of sociopathy. Clinically defined, a sociopath, is someone who has a pervasive pattern of disregard for and violation of the rights of others; fails to conform to social norms with respect to lawful behaviors; is deceptive, as indicated by repeatedly lying, use of aliases, or conning others for personal profit or pleasure; impulsiveness or failure to plan ahead; reckless disregard for safety of self or others; consistent irresponsibility, including repeated failure to honor financial obligations; lack of remorse, as indicated by being indifferent to or rationalizing having hurt, mistreated, or stolen from another. (*Diagnostic and Statistical Manual of Mental Disorders*, 2000)

In strict clinical terms, sociopathy has its origins in early childhood. Yet what we see in the dominant culture is a form of induced sociopathy. This type of sociopath is not likely to seek psychotherapy, let alone pursue a spiritual path. It is unrealistic at best to expect the sociopath to have empathy for the plight of the hard-pressed working person.

Given this appalling reality, a shift in societal behavior can come only from people who have no choice but to fight back against exploitation and impoverishment at the hand of the government and ruling elites.

Transformation

At a certain point, there are enough people with little or nothing to lose to where the fight begins in earnest – the fight for a new society. The needed changes will not likely come in the form of a centralized revolutionary movement, which movements have had their day. The transformations will need to be a combination of centralized organizations and decentralized non-pyramidal organizations. American historian, former government official, and professor of political economy at University of Maryland, Gar Alperovitz, describes the transformation to come as "evolutionary reconstruction." Institutional structures and power will be transformed. As well, there will be the emergence of the new in the interstices – in the cracks – in the old society. There will likely be growing participation in local and grassroots organizations, reliance upon the non-corporate-controlled media (primarily the Internet), and the forming of more workers' cooperatives wherever this is still possible. Perhaps there will even be the movement of entire countries away from systems geared to profit, accumulation, and exponential economic growth and toward a steady-state economy.

Although globalization may be here to stay, it does have some significant vulnerabilities. For one, it is wholly dependent on working people producing value, consuming goods and paying taxes. The fact that the United States and mega-corporations are premised on the need to grow their power and profits, rather than on providing quality of life and security for working people, ensures that they are increasingly viewed as parasitical, authoritarian, and as enemies of the common people. And even in a numb and stupefied populace, desperation, anger and opposition will continue to mount.

Still, without a clearly stated positive alternative, people are easily manipulated by well-funded corporate media campaigns, phony grass-roots organizations funded by secretive billionaires (such as the Koch brothers), and demagogic political hacks. Without a common vision, opposition to Superpower corporatism and globalism is incoherent and ultimately devolves, becoming disintegrative, anarchic and reactionary.

Clearly visible on the horizon are all the elements needed for a radically transformed society. Such a society will need to transcend the contradictions of our current dying political and economic systems. And increasingly, around the globe, people are embracing new ideas and ways of living, pointing the direction to a sustainable future for humanity.

CHAPTER 17.

THE FUTURE IS ALREADY HAPPENING

Let the Real Work Begin

If we, as a nation, commit to doing our work right and also the right work, we might decide there are lots of jobs that don't need to be done or shouldn't be done. We might see that many industries are obsolete or obsolescing, and that others need re-purposing. We would work together to create jobs we do need, and to find ways to pay for them – such jobs as providing nutritious food, excellent education and construction of non-polluting transportation systems. Indeed, our potential as human beings will be realized, through doing the right work, as well as by uplifting each other through loving and respectful relationships.

If we want progressive change, we first must accurately analyze the ills besetting our society. Even more important, we must envision a positive replacement for the old, and now corrupt, order.

The vision, or blueprint for our revamped society, must incorporate the right to fair pay, clean air, water, and food, as well as educational opportunities and affordable health care. However, none of these basic rights will be preserved unless and until it is understood that the role of government is to ensure these basic rights are preserved.

Investing in education, health, infrastructure, green-tech, and environmental sustainability make sense economically and is, in fact, crucial to our survival. Government can institute policies to support these kinds of investments.

Everywhere, seeds of a new society are germinating and sprouting. Working models are thriving, as are a growing number of egalitarian, often green, worker-owned cooperatives. Even some unions are considering alternatives to the "growth at any cost" model of capitalism. United Steelworkers, for example, signed an agreement with Mondragon Corporation in 2009 to collaborate in establishing unionized cooperatives based on the Mondragon model in manufacturing here and in Canada.

The New Economy Movement

One of the growing progressive movements in the United States is the "New Economy Movement." Involved citizens are working to create a green and socially responsible economy, one that rethinks both the nature of ownership and the growth paradigm that currently rules conventional policies. According to Gar Alperovitz, this movement includes numerous egalitarian, and often green, worker-owned cooperatives. He writes,

> Hundreds of 'social enterprises' that use profits for environmental, social or community-serving goals are also

expanding rapidly. In many communities urban agricultural efforts have made common cause with groups concerned with healthy non-processed food. And all this is to say nothing of 1.6 million nonprofit corporations that often cross over into economic activity.

Further, Alperovitz writes that for-profits have also developed alternatives:

There are, for example, more than 11,000 companies owned entirely or in significant part by some 13.6 million employees. Most have adopted Employee Stock Ownership Plans; these so-called ESOPs democratize ownership, though only some of them involve participatory management....

In certain states, companies that want to brandish their new-economy values can now also register as B Corporations. B Corp registration (the "B" stands for "benefit") allows a company to subordinate profits to social and environmental goals. Without this legal authorization, a CEO could in theory be sued by stockholders if profit-making is not his sole objective. Such status insures that specific goals are met by different companies (manufacturers have different requirements from retail stores)....

Cooperatives may not be a new idea – with 130 million members-plus (more than one in three Americans), co-ops have broad political and cultural support – but they are becoming increasingly important in new-economy efforts. (Alperovitz 2011)

Within the New Economy Movement, working groups are formulating initiatives and creating detailed designs for state and local banks to support the new economy institutional development. (The Bank of North Dakota stands as one important precedent.) The New Economy Working Group is a joint venture between the Institute for Policy Studies (IPS) and *YES! Magazine*. Its overriding goal is to advance a coherent vision of an economy organized around sustainable local community economies.

Alperovitz believes this movement will gather substantial momentum over time. One reason is obvious, he says:

> As citizen uprisings from Tunisia to Madison, Wisconsin, remind us, judgments that serious change cannot take place often miss the quiet buildup of potentially explosive underlying forces of change. Nor were the eruptions of many other powerful movements – from late nineteenth-century populism to civil rights to feminism and gay rights – predicted by those who viewed politics only through the narrow prism of the current moment. (Alperovitz 2011)

Nonprofits also are growing in number. According to American economist Jeremy Rifkin,

> Nonprofits employ nearly 56 million full-time equivalent workers or an average of 5.6 percent of the economically active populations in 42 counties surveyed. The nonprofit workforce now exceeds the workforce in each of the

traditional market sectors in the nations studied, including construction, transport, utilities, communications, and most of the industrial manufacturing industries. The growth in the nonprofit sector is highest in Europe, which now even exceeds the United States. An impressive 15.9 percent of the paid employment in the Netherlands is now in the nonprofit sector. In Belgium, 13.1 percent of all workers are in the nonprofit field, while in the United Kingdom it is 11 percent, in Ireland 10.9 percent, and in France 9 percent of total employment. In the United States, 9.2 percent of the employment is in the nonprofit sector, and in Canada, it is 12.3 percent. (Rifkin 2011)

Collectively owned businesses are also increasing in number. According to Alperovitz,

There are now also more than eleven thousand businesses owned in whole or part by their employees; five million more individuals are involved in these enterprises than are members of private-sector unions. Another 130 million Americans are members of various urban, agricultural, and credit union cooperatives. In many cities, important new 'land trust' developments are underway using an institutional form of nonprofit or municipal ownership that develops and maintains low- and moderate-income housing.

Significantly, these collectively owned businesses are commonly supported by unusual local alliances, including not only progressives, labor unions, and nonprofit and religious leaders, but also, in many cases, the backing of local businesses and bankers." (Alperovitz 2011)

[author's note: For a full list and description of all the New Economy Movement efforts and programs of note, as well as theoretical considerations, see the Alperovitz article in The Nation Magazine, *June 13, 2011, referenced in the bibliography.]*

In developing countries farmers are organizing their own communities and profitably growing organic produce, relinquishing their dependency on expensive imports. They are aligning with partners in the United States and Europe to secure "fair trade" agreements. A Massachusetts-based cooperative, Equal Exchange, currently works with small farmer cooperatives in Africa, Asia, Latin America and the United States. Such cooperatives are owned and governed democratically by the farmers themselves. Their vision is "to create and foster a deep and far reaching cooperative model, with Equal Exchange serving as the engine of a complex economic network of two million producers, workers, investors, merchants, activists, and consumers who are using their land, labor, capital and votes to create the world they want to live in and leave for their children." (Equal Exchange 2011)

La Vía Campesina, a global peasant-farmer organization, is promoting new forms of ecological agriculture, as are Cuba, Venezuela and Brazil's MST (Movimento dos Trabalhadores Rurais Sem Terra).

Architects for some time have been designing sustainable communities. Fred Magdoff, professor emeritus of plant and soil science, and John Bellamy Foster, editor of *Monthly Review* and professor of sociology, sum up the ideal in designs for sustainable communities and transportation systems:

> Concretely, people need to live closer to where they work, in ecologically designed housing built for energy efficiency as well as comfort, and in communities designed for public engagement, with sufficient places, such as parks and community centers, for coming together and recreation opportunities. Better mass transit within and between cities is needed to lessen the dependence on the use of the cars and trucks. Rail is significantly more energy efficient than trucks in moving freight (413 miles per gallon fuel per ton versus 155 miles for trucks) and causes fewer fatalities, while emitting lower amounts of greenhouse gases. One train can carry the freight of between 280 to 500 trucks. And it is estimated that one rail line can carry the same amount of people as numerous highway lanes. Industrial production needs to be based on ecological design principles of "cradle-to-cradle," where products and buildings are designed for lower energy input, relying to as great degree as possible on natural lighting and heating/cooling, ease of construction as well as easy reuse, and ensuring that the manufacturing process produces little to no waste. (Magdoff and Foster 2010).

For several decades environmental organizations have been amassing extensive knowledge bases for how we can cooperate with nature. The community-supported agriculture movement (CSA) is spread-ing. Scientists and engineers are applying their best expertise to restoring wetlands. Local community and state banks are being created, to step away from the global financial system with its increasingly speculative investments and false valuations. These alternative banks keep wealth more closely linked to the real value of what's produced, whether in the community or the state. Companies producing real value – intrinsic value rather than speculative value – are doing well. These include solar power companies and organic foods producers. (A partial list of projects and companies engaged in innovative work that supports sustainability and creating what is of real value, can be found in Notes, Chapter 17: Visionary Environmentally-Conscious Companies and Projects.)

According to Christopher Swan, a San Francisco-based visionary and specialist in infrastructure and transportation, nearly all of the technology we need for massive infrastructure transformation is on the market now. What is needed is more investments to be made in these transformations. He writes,

We have now the technology whereby buildings can be powered by solar-panel roofing; railways can return; dams can be removed and rivers restored. It's happening now.

Opportunities in new infrastructure are up, way up compared to any previous moment in the history of industrialization. Millions of people, in the US and

worldwide, are not wasting a minute of their time envisioning the apocalypse *du jour;* rather they have been quietly
developing innumerable new technologies and political
initiatives to create new forms of infrastructure. They
are focused primarily on five areas of new infrastructure
technology – energy, water, mobility, agriculture and
ecological restoration. The results are a host of tools that
promise huge reductions in all resource use, the end of
pollution and the restoration of wild environments.

Today's infrastructure pioneers have conceived a
family of technologies and land use strategies that represent
the paradox: a decrease in resources, yet increase in quality
of life.

Today's new infrastructure technologies clearly
demonstrate that humanity can live very well on far less
of all resources, yet with ample clean energy, water and
food. It is technically and economically feasible to build
all sorts of structures powered by solar technologies on
private rooftops and walls, structures that are constructed of
all sustainable materials and use less than 5% the water of
conventional structures, relying primarily on rain. It is also
feasible to produce vehicles entirely of recyclable materials,
all powered by renewable energy. Such technologies either
exist or are under development now by entrepreneurs and
major corporations.

The evidence all points to the beginnings of an
infrastructure revolution of unprecedented scale and scope.

Global electrification, of homes, industry and transportation, with no air or water pollution, is now possible for the first time. The implications are rising living standards, declining disease, restoration of the planet, declining greenhouse gases and an explosion of creativity.

This seeming utopia is not emerging just because it is altruistic, nor even because any political body offers such a policy. This revolution is happening because it increases quality of life, because it represents global commercial potentials measured in the trillions of dollars, and because it has already started. (Swan 2011, 2007)

Communication technologies are linking us together as a world community as never before. Internet technology is being used to create an infrastructure of distributed green energy grids. Working with several local and national governments, Jeremy Rifkin is promoting the vision and implementation of what he terms the Third Industrial Revolution. Germany and the European Union have been taking the lead in this effort. Rifkin writes,

In the coming era, hundreds of millions of people will produce their own green energy in their homes, offices, and factories and share it with each other in an "energy Internet," just like we now create and share information online. The democratization of energy will bring with it a fundamental reordering of human relationships, impacting the very way we conduct business, govern society, educate our children, and engage in civic life.

The forty-year build-out of the TIR infrastructure will create hundreds of thousands of new businesses and hundreds of millions of new jobs. Its completion will signal the end of a two-hundred-year commercial saga characterized by industrious thinking, entrepreneurial markets, and mass labor workforces and the beginning of a new era marked by collaborative behavior, social networks, and boutique professional and technical workforces. In the coming half century, the conventional, centralized business operations of the First and Second Industrial Revolutions will increasingly be subsumed by the distributed business practices of the Third Industrial Revolution; and the traditional, hierarchical organization of economic and political power will give way to lateral power organized nodally across society. (Rifkin 2011)

This is but a brief summary of the positive changes emerging throughout the world. Counterpoint to the chaos and destruction we are experiencing now, this also is a time of great transition. As we advance to the next promising phase, the opportunity for abundant joy, health and sufficiency of material goods produced in an environmentally sustainable way is increasing.

If abundance can be accurately defined as having what we want as well as what we need, then the time is nearing for us all to experience, indeed revel in, increased abundance.

Conclusion

The heart's deepest wisdom knows the simple truth that what is good for ourselves, each other, all of life and the planetary systems is that which supports life. True heart's desire is not concerned with ideologies or religion or politics. It is concerned with the most potent way we can love ourselves and one another.

As humans we possess the creativity and resources to evolve continually. For some, this may take the form of inventing refined techniques and technologies for producing material wealth. For others, evolution might mean developing intelligence, relationship skills and understanding. For others, attainment of improved health might be the goal. Whatever the form or focus, any evolutionary step will be greatly enhanced if we honor our true nature, and respect ourselves and others as integral and essential parts of All That Is.

Being enslaved to what others think we should be, want and feel keeps us from our true nature and our connection to the biosphere. Nature has its own intelligence which is far superior to the designs of mankind, and we ignore it at our peril.

During the years ahead, it will seem to many that the world as we all once knew it is coming to an end, that these are the prophesied "End Times." Yet rather than an end, we will be experiencing a profound transformation as the old order, the outmoded and unworkable civilization, unravels, to be replaced by new livelihoods, new forms of government, new consciousness that enables and allows the restoration of ethics, morality and loving service to all... including our natural world.

As spiritual beings, we stand as part of the interconnected biosphere and All That Is. If we translate it into love for one another, it becomes the ground for our most inspired contributions. Through direct connection to Inner Guidance, or God, as befits your beliefs, you can receive guidance in every aspect of life, and direction in how to navigate the shoals and make a life that works. Intuition, openness to inspiration and Inner Guidance is the gate through which you must walk. In so doing you will access the vital role you can play in the great transformation unfolding before us.

May you enjoy the journey.

About the Author

Karen McChrystal, MA, is an interdisciplinary researcher and author. She is the Publisher and Editor-in-Chief for Quantum Era Press, based in Santa Monica, California, which provides all prepress services to independent authors. She is also the Executive Director and a founder of the Sustainable Living Institute, a non-profit organization based in Santa Monica, California.

Her undergraduate studies were done at Stanford University, where she received a BA in political science. She completed a Master's degree in Clinical Psychology at the Western Institute for Social Research, in San Francisco, California.

After graduating with a BA, she worked as an investigative journalist and was an editor/managing editor for various print publications. After receiving her Master's degree, she had a successful private practice as a psychotherapist for thirteen years, then quit to be able to do something different – first to pursue environmentalism, then to work in the Internet industry as editor for online publications. For the past twelve years, as owner of Quantum Era Press, she has been helping other authors publish their own books.

Every creature is full of God
And is a book about God.
Every creature is a word of God.

All creatures flow outward, but nonetheless
  remain within God.
Everything that is in God, is God.
God is a being beyond Being and a Nothingness
  beyond Being.
God's being is my being
And God's primordial being
Is my primordial being.

Because this Word is a hidden Word.
It comes in the darkness of the night.
To enter this darkness put away
All voices and sounds
All images and likenesses
In stillness and peace
In this unknowing knowledge
God speaks in the soul.

~ *Meister Eckhart*, translated by Mathew Fox

NOTES

CHAPTER 11

DESUBLIMATION:

As described by Herbert Marcuse,

> "Desublimation is obviously so powerful that even a small
> dose can succeed in capturing us. We will return repetitively to
> satisfy ourselves even in small ways. As an example, something
> like *Playboy* magazine could be allowed to feed men a measure
> of unusual – that is, formerly tabooed – sexual satisfaction,
> but this would happen only by becoming a regular buying
> customer. When one turned to look at American society of the
> 60s, it was clear that sexuality was being desublimated in a
> variety of ways so long as people were ready to consume the
> right things. Thus, people were actually being repressed anew
> to the specific advantages of capitalist producers. Looking at
> American society, today, little has changed, I would say. We
> have become progressively more narrow (repressed) in our
> satisfaction of even recreation! We are being convinced that
> we can buy it in the form of ever-more-expensive mountain
> clothing or recreational vehicles. Meanwhile, most people who
> buy mountain clothing and four-wheel-drive vehicles never go
> to the mountains. We have become implicitly convinced (and
> victimized), believing that recreation is achieved in the purchase
> and ownership itself. This after all is what capitalism requires
> – a never-ending will to consume products." (Marcuse, www4.
> hmc.edu:8001/Humanities/Beckman/PhilNotes/marcuse.htm)

The world of objects and relations between things spring into a kind of
life of their own, within the movement of commodities through the market
system. Even when economists gradually discover the laws governing

these objects, they still appear to have an invisible force, generating their own power. An individual aware of these laws is still unable to modify the process by his own activity. His activity itself becomes estranged from him as it is turned into a commodity which is also subject to the non-human laws of the marketplace.

Not only is the worker separated from any meaningful relationship to the product of his labor, his labor itself has become increasingly fragmented through the Taylorization* of white-collar as well as of blue-collar jobs. Work is reduced to the mechanical repetition of increasingly specialized sets of actions; the worker becomes the "mass worker," indifferent to the particular content of the job, because it is all equally meaningless, except for the price paid for the work and the pleasantness, however shallow, of the company of co-workers.

TAYLORIZATION:

Taylorization means the breaking down of complex, multiple job operations which require a variety of skills into the simplest possible components, each carried out by a single worker, such that skill, and thus control of the work process, is effectively taken out of the hands of the worker and concentrated in the hands of management. For an account of this process, see Braverman, Harry, *Labor and Monopoly Capital*, especially Chapter 4, "Scientific Management."

The fragmentation of the process of production necessarily entails the fragmentation of its subject. In consequence of the technical rationalization of the work-process, the human qualities and idiosyncrasies of the worker appear increasingly as mere sources of error when contrasted with these abstract special laws functioning according to rational predictions. Man is no longer the authentic master of the process; on the contrary, he is a mechanical part incorporated into a mechanical system. (Lukacs, 1971)

Denied any active role for his intelligence, apart from creative adaptation, rebellion, or organized opposition, his creative powers of cognition are largely suppressed, as is his will. He is forced into an increasingly contemplative or neurotic position. And to assert an individual distinction of character or to suggest that the inner self is constantly changing, is to experience a threat to ones identity as part of the outer world and its laws of the market.

CHAPTER 12 CAPITAL

Capital is minimally defined by Karl Marx as accumulated labor power, or the congealed historic relationships between those who own the means of production and those who sell their labor to them. More concretely, capital can take many forms: stock certificates, fixed plant, inventories of commodities awaiting sale, and so on. But the heart of the congealed relationships is productive wage labor: wage workers are productive in the capitalist sense when they produce in their day's work a value of commodities which is greater than the value of their day's wages. This greater value, surplus value, is realized as profit through the sale of the commodities and reinvested as new raw materials, fixed plant, and workers. But capital exists only as many capitals – fixed, circulating, and constant – e.g., firms, industries, whole national economies. Each capital is driven to maximize surplus value, to grow, by the pressure of competition from others. Capital as a whole is thus inherently expansionist. It tends to dominate more and more of the world and convert more and more people into wage workers and commodity consumers. Through the commodities its workers produce, capital penetrates all aspects of social life and transforms them according to its own blind, flatly quantitative needs.

Hungarian Marxist scholar and literary critic, Georg Lukacs, further explains,

> It is the order of the marketplace, which changes all qualities into quantities and judges their worth according to yet another quantity – the price thereto affixed. Likewise, human beings are judged only according to the contribution they make to the accumulation of global capital.
> ...What circulates through this global organization of the world of quantities, the objective world, is not predominantly human

creativity, but rather the exchange of commodities. Social relations are subordinated to and concealed by the latter.

...In this situation a man's own activity, his own labor, becomes something objective and independent of him, something that controls him by virtue of an autonomy alien to man.

(Lukacs 1971)

CHAPTER 14: GMO FOODS.

"GMO versus Organics: Thirty years of GMOs
Are More Than Enough,"
by Mae Wan Ho

Summarizing the detriments of using GMO seeds and crops, Mae Wan Ho writes,

- No increase in yields; on the contrary GM soya decreased yields by up to 20 percent compared with non-GM soya [4], and up to 100 percent failures of Bt cotton have been recorded in India [6]. New studies confirmed these findings. Research from the University of Kansas found a 10 percent yield drag for Roundup Ready soya [9] that required extra manganese applied to the soil to make up the yield deficit. A team of scientists from the USDA and the University of Georgia found growing GM cotton in the US could result in a drop in income by up to 40 percent [10, 11] (Transgenic Cotton Offers No Advantage, SiS 38)

- No reduction in pesticides use; on the contrary, USDA data showed that GM crops increase pesticide use by 50 million pounds from 1996 to 2003 in the United States [4]. New data paint an even grimmer picture: the use of glyphosate on major crops went up more than 15-fold between 1994 and 2005, along with increases in other herbicides [12] in order to cope with rising glyphosate resistant superweeds [6]. Roundup tolerant canola volunteers are top among the worries of Canadian farmers [13, 14] (Study Based on Farmers' Experience Exposes Risks of GM Crops, SiS 38) Roundup herbicide is lethal to frogs and toxic to human placental and embryonic cells [6]. Roundup is used in more than 80 percent of all GM crops planted in the world.

- GM crops harm wildlife, as revealed by UK's farm scale evaluations [6], and more recently in a study led by Loyola University, Chicago, Illinois in the United Stated, which found that wastes from Bt corn impaired the growth of a common aquatic insect [15, 16] (Bt Crops Threaten Aquatic Ecosystems, SiS 36)

- Bt resistant pests and Roundup tolerant superweeds render the two major GM crop traits practically useless [6]. A recent review concluded that [17] "evolved glyphosate-resistant weeds are a major risk for the continued success of glyphosate and transgenic glyphosate-resistant crops." And the evolution of Bt resistant bollworms worldwide have now been confirmed and documented in more than a dozen fields in Mississippi and Arkansas between 2003 and 2006 [18]

- Vast areas of forests, pampas and cerrados lost to GM soya in Latin America, 15 m hectares in Argentina alone [6]; and this has worsened considerably with the demand for biofuels.

- Epidemic of suicides in the cotton belt of India involving 100 000 farmers between 1993-2003, and a further 16 000 farmers a year have died since Bt cotton was introduced [6]

- Transgene contamination unavoidable, scientists find GM pollination of non-GM crops and wild relatives 21 kilometres away [19]

- GM food and feed linked to deaths and sicknesses both in the fields in India and in lab tests around the world (more below)

There is ample scientific research proving that organically grown crops give higher yield, organic produce is more nutritious, and organic plants are more disease resistant. (Ho and Burcher 2008)

Genetic engineering of plants and animals began in the mid 1970s in the belief that the genome (the totality of all the genetic material of a species) is constant and static, and that the characteristics of organism are simply hardwired in their genome. But geneticists soon discovered that the genome is remarkably dynamic and 'fluid', and constantly in conversation with the environment. This determines which genes are turned on, when, where, by how much and for how long. Moreover, the genetic material itself could also be marked or changed according to experience, and the influence passed on to the next generation. (Ho 2008)

Resistant weeds so far cover over 4.5 million hectares in the US alone, while world-wide coverage is thought to have reached at least 120 million hectares by 2010. The US has the worst problem, with 13 different species in 73 different locations. Palmer amaranth now infests over 1 million separate sites in North Carolina alone, while Horseweeds have infested 100,000 sites in Delaware. In Argentina, 100,000 acres of soya crop lands is now infested with Johnson Grass. (Sirinathsinghji 2011)

CHAPTER 15

OFFSHORING:

"How Offshoring Has Destroyed the Economy,"
by Paul Craig Roberts, American economist, formerly Assistant Secretary of the Treasury in the Reagan Administration.

Paraphrasing from the Council on Foreign Relations report of March 2011, Roberts writes,

[But] with engineering, design, and research jobs offshored, and with many of the jobs that remain within the US filled by foreigners on HB-1 and L-1 visas, we now have the phenomenon of American university and college graduates, heavily indebted with student loans, jobless, and living with their parents, who support them.

[Some] economists, especially those high profile ones in high profile academic institutions, were bought and paid for. In exchange for grants from offshoring corporations these hirelings invented "the New Economy," in which everyone would prosper as a result of getting rid of "dirty fingernail jobs."

The New Economy wouldn't make anything, but it would lead the world in innovation and in financing what others did make. The "new economists" were not sufficiently bright to realize that if a country didn't make anything, it couldn't innovate.

Spence [in the CFR report] also acknowledges that the change in the structure of American employment from higher productivity to lower productivity jobs is the reason both for the stagnation in US consumer income and for the rising inequality of income. Sending middle class jobs abroad raised the earnings of capital. Spence understands that the lack of growth in consumer income has resulted in a shortfall in domestic demand, resulting in high unemployment.

He could have added that offshoring jobs also gave us the Federal Reserve's policy of pumping up consumer debt as a substitute for the missing growth in consumer income. There is an obvious limit to the ability to maintain the growth of consumer demand via the growth of indebtedness.

The offshored economy is the "New Economy," which the "free trade" hirelings of Wall Street and the global corporations invented in order to pay, with grants from the offshoring corporations, for their summer homes in the Hamptons. (Roberts 2011)

CHAPTER 16: MONDRAGON

(Excerpted with permission from *The Next Evolution: A Blueprint for Transforming the Planet*, by Jack Reed, Community Planet Foundation, 2001, p. 88.)

The [Mondragon] cooperative started in 1956 in the village of Mondragon, manufacturing two products with 24 workers. By 1959 they had jobs for one hundred people. Their firm was modeled after the successful 1844 Rochdale cooperative in England which flourished until it opened itself to more capital participants who outvoted the original group and took control. Within three years the Rochdale company then became an ordinary capitalist firm.

However, the Mondragon co-op model proved to be so successful that, in less than 30 years, it grew from one cooperative with 25 workers to more than 100 worker cooperatives with 19,500 workers in the region.[27] [ff. 27: Whyte, William and Kathleen, Making Mondragon: *The Growth and Dynamics of the Worker Cooperative Complex,* ILC Press, Cornell University, Ithaca, New York: 1988, p. 5.] This was made possible by starting cooperative banks which mobilized small reserves enabling the local coops to be financed. Because the goal was for *everyone* to succeed, the banks would meet with prospective new co-ops and help them succeed. They would help find land, supplies, a market for the products, personnel, training, etc. They would also do feasibility studies, monitor progress, and make up one-third of the coop's board of directors. The system proved so successful that only 3 of the 103 worker cooperatives created between 1956 and 1986 were shut down.[28] [ff. 28: Whyte, p. 5.] Compare that with what we know about starting businesses in the everyone-for-themselves paradigm. Since only 20 percent of our new businesses survive even five years, Mondragon's survival rate of more than 97 percent across three decades indeed commands attention.[29] [ff. 29: Whyte, pg. 5.]

Since the cooperatives were worker owned, the Spanish government would not help with welfare, medical care, etc. No problem. The co-ops created their own co-op social security and healthcare. They even built a co-op hospital and a co-op university where the students worked and produced products and owned the co-op. Many of the supermarkets and schools also became cooperatives. Because housing was expensive, they built co-op housing owned by the tenants.

How successful are these worker-owned coop-eratives? The productivity of the Mondragon co-op workers is the highest in Spain, higher than the most successful capitalist firms, and the net profit on sales is twice as high as the most profitable capitalist firms. The Basque region never received nor had to depend on outside investment capital to get started or to expand their businesses.

The reason for the success of the now prosperous Mondragon region is that the people decided to pool their resources and make it work for everyone. Because managers and workers both knew that they served each other's interests, they could move ahead boldly with an unusual degree of agreement. Since they lived in the same villages, no differences were perceived between managers and workers. They limited the co-ops to 500 members (beyond which they split up and formed a new co-op) because they found that co-ops couldn't operate beyond that number. This helped maintain a family feeling. The now prosperous Mondragon region is an example of people working together for the mutual benefit of all. Had the everyone-for-themselves paradigm been in effect instead, the result probably would have been that a few people gathered most of the money while the majority of the people would still be living in poverty in the region.

CHAPTER 17

VISIONARY ENVIRONMENTALLY-CONSCIOUS COMPANIES AND PROJECTS:

(list courtesy of Christopher Swan)

Elwha River Restoration Project: Elwha Dam Removal. Courtesy of Olympic National Park. This is happening now. A phenomenal process with huge implications – placing the value of wildlife and fish stocks over archaic energy-generation systems. YouTube: www.youtube.com/watch?v=dKGlt00PVzE.

Bloom Energy: "Be The Solution." Bloom Energy is a leading maker of fuel cells, based in Silicon Valley, California, with products used by Google and others to generate electricity from natural gas. www.bloomenergy.com.

Calera: This company figured out how to sequester carbon dioxide exhaust from power plants by making it into cement! Hence the C of CO2 becomes concrete highways and railroad ties and so on. www.calera.com.

Ceramic Fuel Cells Limited: "Fuel Cells." This technology is a curious and wonderful breakthrough in fuel cell structure, whereby the cell becomes little more than a flat wafer that receives hydrogen gas from any source and turns it into electricity. The point is that this new tech is doing to propulsion and power systems what the microprocessor did to computers. www.cfcl.com.au/Fuel_Cells/.

Eco-Structure Magazine: Improving environmental performances of buildings and their surroundings. Published by the American Institute of Architects, this is a great source for getting a feel for new trends and new technology. Also see Landscape Architecture magazine, as it has many inspiring stories on restoration. Graphically, a feast for the eyes. www.eco-structure.com/.

Elwha River Restoration Project: Elwha Dam Removal, Courtesy of Olympic National Park. This is happening now. A phenomenal process with huge implications – placing the value of wildlife and fish stocks over archaic energy-generation systems. YouTube: www.youtube.com/watch?v=dKGlt00PVzE.

EV World: Driving the Electric Future in Motion Since 1998. Compendium of various products. Suffice it to say, this is a catalog of innovation in the field in the US. www.evworld.com/index.cfm.

Metropolis Magazine: "Lessons of Place." by Susan S. Szenasy. This article typifies a trend in considerations about place – where we live – and how many people and groups are involved in improving their place and largely ignoring larger politics. The magazine is a treasure trove of innovative ideas in living, working and designing. www.metropolismag.com/story/20111115/lessons-of-place. November 15, 2011.

Nocera Lab: Research Group of Daniel G. Nocera. This scientist is now commercializing a new form of electrolyzer that more efficiently produces hydrogen from water. The work is a breakthrough in hydrogen energy solutions. http://nocera.mit.edu/Home.

Sanyo's Aqua: "Wash Clothes Without Water." Sanyo's new washing machine, the Aqua AWD-AQ1, can clean your clothes without water. Oxygen in the air is converted to ozone, using an ozone creation device, and is sprayed on clothing inside the drum. Ozone has a strong oxidation action, which either destroys or disassembles the cell walls of bacteria. This allows for eliminating bacteria, odors, and dirt (organic matter).

This product, one of several now on the market outside the US, has far reaching implications in terms of reducing water use and runoff of detergent into the watershed www.treehugger.com/gadgets/sanyos-aqua-wash-clothes-without-water.html. (February 6, 2006)

Solar Lighting: Piped Daylighting Systems. The wonderful world of light transmitted by fiber optics. Or, sunlight in the basement! www.fsec.ucf.edu/en/consumer/buildings/basics/windows/solar_lighting/piped.htm.

Turner Ranches: With approximately two million acres of personal and ranch land, Ted Turner is the second largest individual landholder in North America. Turner lands are innovatively managed and work to partner economic viability with ecological sustainability. All Turner ranches operate as working businesses, relying on bison and outfitting as principal enterprises. In addition, Turner ranches support many progressive environmental projects including water resource management, reforestation and the reintroduction of native species to the land.

Land and watershed restoration is a huge realm of work. Ted Turner is perhaps the biggest player, managing over 50,000 head of bison and 18 ranches. www.tedturner.com/ranches.asp.

Urban Design Tools: Low Impact Development. "Permeable Pavers." Here is a collection of ideas for a really boring product with great significance And that's the point: even really basic things you never think about are changing and benefitting the environment in significant ways. www.lid-stormwater.net/permpavers_benefits.htm.

APPENDIX

THE BREATH OF LIFE: A PATH TO INNER PEACE

This particular breath method derives from the breathing method originally developed by the late Maurice Rowdon. His background was in Pranayama Yoga and the traditions of Ramana Maharshi and Yogananda. Having spent ten years working with Mr. Rowdon and learning from him, I then developed the method further and employed it with patients in my psychotherapy practice in the 1980's and early 1990's. The late-Mr. Rowdon had called his method Oxygenesis™. I've called my version of the method Alphacentrics™. It had been my experience that the method was most effectively practiced with a facilitator guiding the person doing the breathing. However, due to the widespread fear and stress inhibiting so many people, and because a text can reach more people, I decided to make this method available via the following text. A careful reading and practice can take the sincere person a long way toward achieving inner peace and toward living a stress-free, inspired life.

THE BREATH OF LIFE: A PATH TO INNER PEACE

Breathing techniques have been used for centuries, all with varying degrees of effectiveness. The Alphacentrics™ method is the most effective for stress elimination, relaxation, healing on all levels, and connecting with one's underlying spiritual essence.

Using the breath, you can get to your peaceful center, which is always there waiting for you. If you practice regularly, you will be able to "breathe" yourself to a place deep inside yourself, where there is no fear, worry, stress, not even pain, hunger or cold. In this place, you will receive higher energies from your individual soul's connection to Spirit. Spirit connection brings healing, love, and knowledge. Spirit is infinite. It is a living Divine Intelligence that is in everything, every molecule, and we are individual expressions of it.

Peacefulness will ultimately take you to the vast loving space of All That Is, and you will remember this is the home you were always meant to return to, to the Source of all Love.

Once you've experienced this a few times, you'll understand the importance of learning to stay peaceful *no matter what*.

How can just breathing do this? Remember, the words inspiration and respiration are closely related. "Inspiration" comes from the Latin word *inspirare*. Spirare means "to breathe," so inspire = to breathe in. "Respiration" comes from the Latin words re+spirare.

Think of the breath as a fuel source for your body, namely oxygen. Our lungs and diaphragm are the billows that feed the fuel of oxygen to all our cells, our blood, to every part of your body.

First, it's important to know that when you breathe in the abdomen, that is, pulling the diaphragm down on the inhale, you turn off the production of stress chemicals.

Secondly, most adults don't get enough oxygen. About 90% of adults are oxygen deficient, because they're stuck in chest-breathing – only breathing high in the chest. The shoulders go up, the chest expands a little, but the lungs don't fully inflate. This gives you only one-fifth or less of the amount of oxygen your lungs were designed to hold.

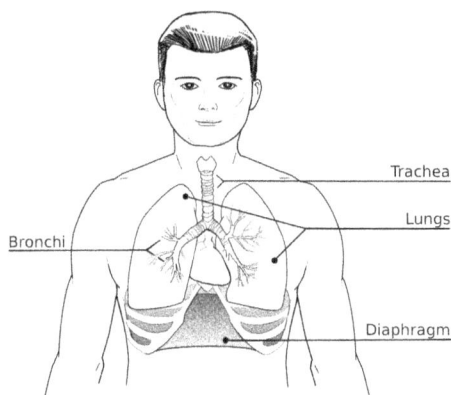

The lungs can hold about two gallons of air, on average. But most people only inhale one-half to two pints, because they breathe high in the chest. The upper part of the lungs is narrower and has less volume than the lower part, as you'll see in the diagram on the left.

If you're oxygen deficient, nothing is going to work right, and you won't experience optimum health. Every cell in your body needs oxygen. Oxygen catalyzes cell metabolism to give us energy, neutralizes toxins, and keeps us resistant to diseases, to name just a few of its important functions.

Healthy babies breathe naturally and easily. Their breath is in the belly or in the chest, depending on what their body needs. And when we fall asleep at night, or when we're truly relaxed, the body reverts to abdominal breathing. But as we go through life, we experience a lot of pressures, stressful situations, maybe trauma. This affects our mental habits, but also creates physical patterns of holding stress, especially in the trunk area. We start to tighten up and get into rigid patterns of breathing that restrict our breath, so we don't get enough oxygen.

Another important thing to understand is that if we're stuck in chest breathing, it will be very difficult not to feel stressed or anxious. Chest breathing tends to keep the stress response stimulated – the "fight or flight response." This produces stress hormones, which produce more anxiety and worry. It's a vicious cycle. And we have to break that cycle.

In our culture most people have gotten used to a level of permanent stress – they don't even realize they're stressed. It's like the fish that doesn't know it's wet. Many people live in a state of perpetual imbalance, caused by stress, and so they get sick and tired.

When the body has to use energy for the stress response, it takes energy away from keeping our immune system healthy, repairing physical damage, preventing degenerative diseases, and keeping digestion and elimination working properly, and replenishing our energy.

We live in a culture with endless pressures and stress. How do we break the cycle and stop worrying and feeling anxious? We can't do too much to eliminate the demands and pressures we face in life, every day, but we can change the way we respond to them. It's a matter of getting back to our center, so we can calmly address the situation and see clearly how to deal with it. Using the breath, we can learn to stay relaxed and peaceful, no matter what. We can be like the calm eye in the center of the tornado.

The good news is, if you just do the breathing exercise, you can get back to peacefulness. I will explain the basic mechanics of breathing, so you can understand how to use your breath to control your reaction to stressors.

Remember, continual chest breathing stimulates the fight-or-flight response. Fight-or-flight is good if we need to fight or to flee, but that doesn't happen very often. Habitual chest breathing keeps adrenaline, or, epinephrine, pumping.

Adrenaline is a "fight or flight" hormone, a major component of the biochemistry of the stress reaction. It's released from the adrenal glands when danger threatens or in an emergency, and we get an adrenaline rush.

The stress response also stimulates the production of sugar, by releasing the hormone cortisol (glucocorticoid), which is a steroid. This is the other main component of the biochemistry of the stress response. If we face an actual emergency, we need that extra sugar to respond to the situation. But most of the time, we're just worrying about things, not fighting or fleeing, so these stress hormones accumulate in the body. The stored sugars can add excess belly fat, and the hormone residue also makes the body pH acidic. Your pH should be slightly alkaline. When it's acidic, the body doesn't work properly and disease and pathogens are invited in. (Cancer, by the way, can survive only in an acidic body; it cannot grow in a properly alkaline body.)

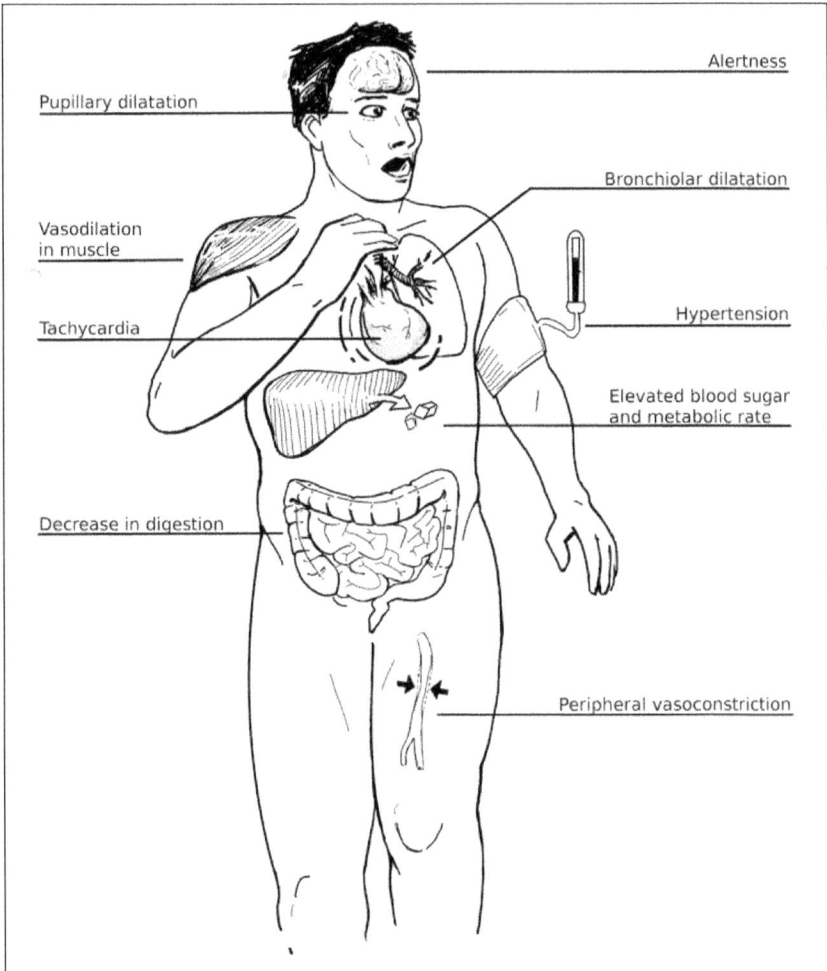

Alertness

Pupillary dilatation

Bronchiolar dilatation

Vasodilation
in muscle

Hypertension

Tachycardia

Elevated blood sugar
and metabolic rate

Decrease in digestion

Peripheral vasoconstriction

How do we stop the stress response?

We can't experience fear or stress if we're not pumping stress hormones – adrenaline and cortisol. Without these hormones – the chemistry for fight or flight – we don't feel like fighting or fleeing, we don't feel needless anxiety, hostility, or paranoia. We become peaceful again.

How do we stop pumping stress hormones?

It's pretty simple, really. We start breathing in the belly. Belly breathing, or abdominal breathing, does two things: it expands the chest cavity, bringing more oxygen into the lungs, in particular, into the lower lobes of the lungs. This way, the body gets enough oxygen to neutralize the accumulated stress hormones.

Belly breathing also stimulates the parasympathetic system and the relaxation response, which stops further production of stress hormones. When the parasympathetic system is on, the sympathetic system is off, and vice versa. You simply cannot have both systems working at once.

When a person is relaxed, their breathing is through the nose, slow, even and gentle, in the belly. Deliberately mimicking a relaxed breathing pattern, breathing in the belly, seems to calm the autonomic nervous system, and we feel relaxed.

What is the relaxation response?

It's what happens when the parasympathetic system is "on." When the parasympathetic nervous system is on, the sympathetic nervous system is off.

Here's what happens in the relaxation response, when the parasympathetic system is on:

- Blood pressure and heart rate are lowered

- The amount of stress hormones is reduced

🦎 Lactic acid build-up in muscle tissue is reduced

🦎 Your pH begins to normalize

🦎 Immune system functioning is improved

🦎 Your body can repair and heal itself

🦎 Your physical energy will increase

🦎 You'll feel calmness and well being

But isn't there a mental part?

Yes, we have to address this also. The mental is the hardest part for most people. But it's easier than you think. All we really have to do is to give the mind something to do other than thinking, worrying or anticipating problems. We give it something mindless to do, so to speak. You can't mentally try to quiet the mind, because the more you think about quieting the mind, the more you think. You can visualize pleasant relaxing nature scenes, but that takes a lot of mental focus and effort. You can repeat affirmations, but they don't really work, except maybe as a method for focusing the mind.

The simplest and most efficient method is to pay attention to the breath. I'll tell you how to do this in a bit.

People often find it's a challenge to get their thoughts to stop.

You'll need to try it, to find out how easy it is. When you're focused on the breath, you won't be likely to get caught up in your thoughts. If you do, just remember to watch the thoughts go by, like so many passing clouds.

With the controlled rhythmic breath, we can accelerate how quickly we work through everything weighing on our mind. The unconscious mind starts helping, and solutions to problems, visions and plans for how to deal with things, will just appear.

Did you know that the conscious mind makes up only about one-tenth of the mind? The pre-conscious mind (or subconscious) and the unconscious mind form the other 90%. This deeper mind is actually quite brilliant, and designed to help you evolve. But you have to give it a chance, by quieting the conscious mind.

The special method, Alphacentrics, is simple to learn, and, of course, you'll improve with practice. You can start with at least ten minutes a day, but you'll probably want to do more. It's best to plan an uninterrupted forty minutes to an hour daily for this "accelerated meditation."

Starting with the ten minutes a day, at least, you begin to quiet the mind, to refresh yourself, and feel better about yourself and life in in general. It may take longer, depending on how stressed you are, perhaps even as much as an hour or an hour and a half.

The secret is, when you are at peace, you'll still do whatever you need to do, only you'll do it easily and more efficiently – you'll be "in the flow," and you'll get out of the habit of stressing.

I recommend doing this exercise on a regular basis. It's like mental housekeeping. Don't let a backlog of unresolved situations build up and weigh you down with stress. It is best to do the breathing exercises every day, or at least every two or three days, to clear your mind, get back to your peaceful center. Most people enjoy doing it, and choose to do it 30 or 40 minutes a day or anytime they're feeling stressed.

Do really healthy people need to do this breathing method?
Alphacentrics is about more than just becoming healthy physically. This special method of using the breath gives you the benefits of meditation, only faster – it's an accelerated meditation.

First the breath works to get you out of stress, make up for any oxygen deficit, and fuel the body's natural healing. Then the extra charge of oxygen is used for evolving you to higher levels and giving you deeper insight. You'll experience emotional issues resolving themselves. Then the extra charge of oxygen and energy moves you toward actualizing your full potential and raising your consciousness.

Here are some of the benefits of regular practice of Alphacentrics:

- You'll get in touch with who you really are – your authentic self, what you really think, feel and want for yourself.

- You'll understand what your life purpose is.

- Because of this focus and alignment with who you truly are, you'll attract into your life everything you need to be fulfilled and to evolve further.

- You'll be able to respond spontaneously and appropriately to any situation.

- You'll have greater adaptability.

- You'll have more clarity and focus.

- You'll more easily be proactive and make your dreams and goals real.

- Your efficiency will increase, and you'll have ease in doing whatever you want to do.

🦋 Your body will be able to heal itself and keep you healthy and resistant to disease.

🦋 Your intelligence will increase. The breath actually changes your brain (as do some meditation techniques, contemplative practices and prayer).

🦋 You'll experience more joyfulness, love & compassion. People who stick with this breathing method learn how to go into bliss.

🦋 By and by, you'll be able to access the infinite mind, or the Quantum Field, or God... It doesn't matter what you call it.

🦋 As you progress further, you'll begin receiving higher energies, from the Divine Source.

Bringing in Higher Energies

PHYSIOLOGY OF THE BREATH: If you understand the physiology, you can do the exercise and receive all the benefits I just outlined, without having to understand anything about spirituality, psychology, philosophy, theology, physics or metaphysics – not that those aren't all good things.

The diagram below illustrates how the sympathetic nervous system is connected with various organs that are involved in the fight or flight response. If you're fighting or fleeing, the basics are all that matter – you need massive oxygen and cortisol for the extra energy, and the blood pressure up to deliver the energy so the muscles respond instantly. Anything nonessential is turned off, like growth, reproduction or tissue repair.

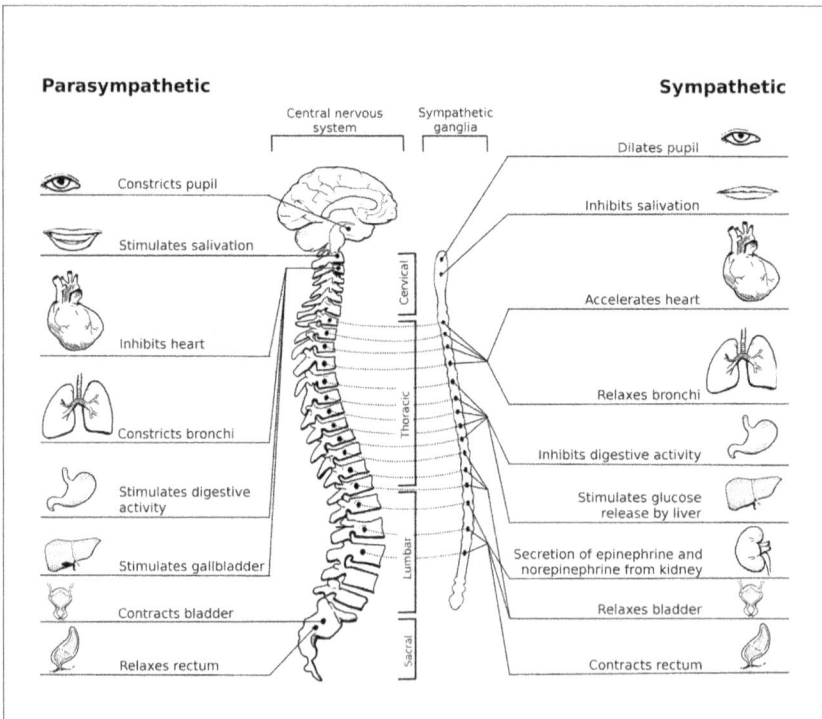

Parasympathetic				Sympathetic
	Central nervous system	Sympathetic ganglia		
Constricts pupil				Dilates pupil
				Inhibits salivation
Stimulates salivation				
		Cervical		Accelerates heart
Inhibits heart				
				Relaxes bronchi
Constricts bronchi		Thoracic		
				Inhibits digestive activity
Stimulates digestive activity				Stimulates glucose release by liver
		Lumbar		Secretion of epinephrine and norepinephrine from kidney
Stimulates gallbladder				
Contracts bladder				Relaxes bladder
		Sacral		
Relaxes rectum				Contracts rectum

If you direct the breath to the upper part of the lungs, it tends to stimulate the sympathetic system; directing the breath to the lower part of the lungs, in abdominal breathing, stimulates the parasympathetic system.

When there isn't any danger, a healthy person returns to homeostasis – the normal state – and the parasympathetic system can be on, doing its job: rest, recuperation, repair, digestion and elimination, and building up your reserves of energy again.

To have proper breathing patterns, you first need flexibility in the diaphragm – the primary muscle of respiration. The diaphragm can get frozen up, especially when people store their emotional tension or stress there. You need to be able to pull the diaphragm down on the inhale.

The diaphragm is shaped like a dome, or a parachute, and is fastened to the bottom of the ribs.

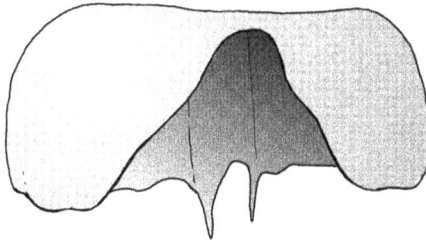

The diaphragm

When the muscles of the diaphragm contract, the dome is flattened, increasing the volume of the chest cavity, pulling in a full breath of air. During controlled belly breathing, the diaphragm muscles contract more forcefully, causing a greater increase in chest volume.

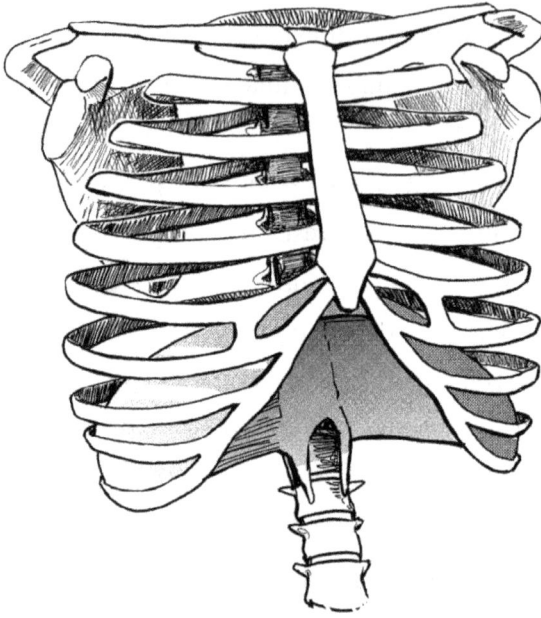

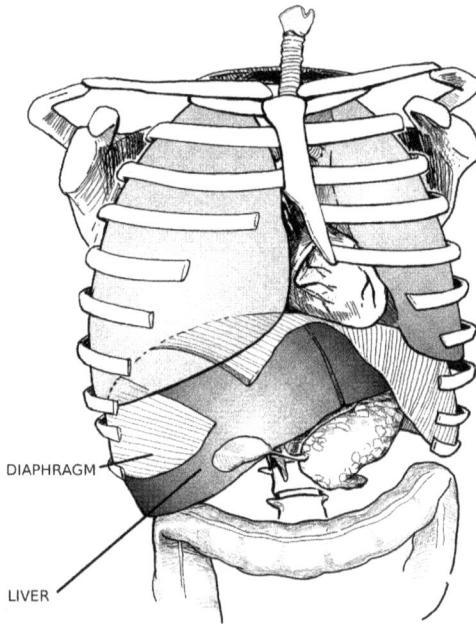

DIAPHRAGM

LIVER

What's loosely referred to as "abdominal breathing" should be thought of more as pulling the diaphragm down, toward the abdomen. When you do this, the belly rises on the inhale. Then you'll feel like you have to also expand your rib cage in order to get a complete breath. Now the diaphragm relaxes a little, as the muscles of the rib cage expand and draw the breath into the upper lungs. This would be a two-part breath, which is a complete breath

In Alphacentrics we use five different breaths, and I'm will teach you the first two – the basic breaths. The first breath to learn is the controlled rhythmic belly breath. Once you know how to use the belly breath and are completely relaxed, you can try the chest breath. The chest breath is a super-charging breath. If you do it when you are completely relaxed, the chest breath will not stimulate the fight-or-flight response.

The other breaths are for more advanced practitioners. Since most people are locked into shallow chest breathing, the belly breath is usually the needed corrective and should be mastered first.

There is a small percentage of people, however – about 10% of the adult population – who are stuck in the belly breath, and don't use the chest breath at all or very little. These people can be less energetic than they'd like to be, uninspired, unmotivated, or even lethargic, or downright depressed. Often their chest will have a collapsed appearance, as if they're discouraged, or resigned, or giving up on life. Or their chest it will look weak and under-developed. These people need to learn the proper way to use the chest breath. It's important to be able do this in order to have extra energy when you need it, like for physical exertion, sports, heavy muscular activity, speaking or singing in public, generally being able to manifest your work in the world, and, of course, for emergency situations.

Once you're breathing correctly, your body will have enough oxygen and energy for its basic physical needs. Alphacentrics breathing brings in an additional charge of oxygen. This oxygen and energy will go where it's next needed, where the body-mind directs it.

It can be to heal an old wound you'd forgotten you had. It can also bring up old memories from the unconscious mind. When this happens, it's actually a healing of old trauma or buried issues. We watch these come up like dream images, and this conscious awareness and the insight it gives are the healing. You don't have to talk it through or analyze it.

Some people receive visions during their breathing sessions. These can hold keys to ones future, or simply offer a better understanding.

Then the breath uses any extra oxygen and energy for evolutionary growth. For an adult, growth comes as higher levels of understanding and higher intelligence – in other words, evolution.

Silent meditation practice will also do this for you, but the Alphacentrics breathing practice will do it faster. It's an accelerated meditation.

The ultimate result of breath- and silence-centered meditations is to move our awareness out of duality and contradiction into a unified understanding and into peacefulness. With practice, we learn to remain peaceful, no matter what. When we're peaceful, we see the path ahead, rather than obstacles in our way. And we can trust our own our inner guidance – our natural wisdom and intuition about what is right for us.

Understanding how to use the breath offers one of the most powerful and effective methods for healing and for raising our consciousness. It's called "the breath of life" for a good reason!

LET'S BEGIN! For most westerners, it's easiest to learn this and practice while lying down, before you expect to be able to do it easily and naturally during normal activities. If you aren't in a place where you can lie down, or you're sitting at your computer, a comfortable sitting position will be fine. You'll need to have a loose waistband, or unfasten your belt.

First try this exercise to get your diaphragm flexible. Take a big breath of air and hold it. Rock this air back and forth between your belly and your chest, as illustrated below.

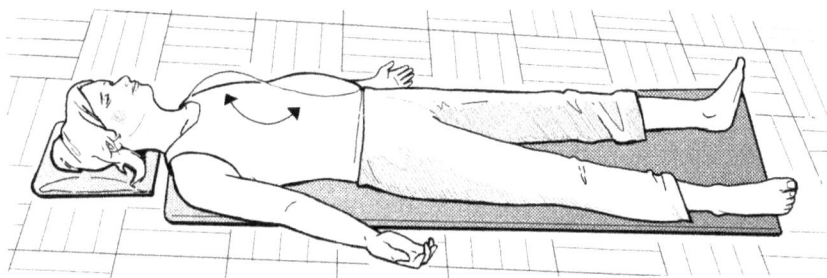

rocking the breath

This may be difficult for some people. A lot of people hold emotional trauma in the diaphragm area. Keep practicing, and you will gain flexibility in the diaphragm, which you need to free the breath to go where it needs to go, naturally.

BELLY BREATH: Next try the belly breath. Belly breathing can be practiced for at least 10 minutes at a time, but it's good to do longer sessions if you can – up to 40 minutes or even an hour, depending on what you feel you need and are able to do. In Alphacentrics, we do all nose breathing. No open-mouthed breathing. Start by inhaling, letting the belly expand, like a balloon. On the exhale, flatten the belly; push out every last drop of air. Then at the end of the exhale, start a new inhale. The bottom of the exhale is a springboard for the inhale. If it helps you, you can put a lightweight book on your belly, and let the belly push it up on the inhale.

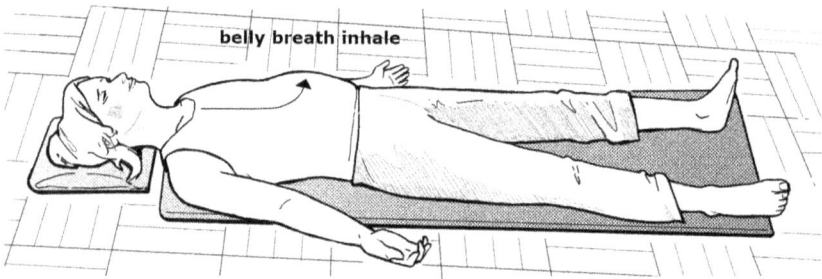
belly breath inhale

Keep the chest from moving. Use a waltz rhythm – inhale for 3 counts; exhale for 3 counts – in-two-three, out-two-three. The speed can vary, depending on how sensitive you are to the additional oxygen. If you feel lightheaded, or your fingers or toes start to curl a little (which is called tetany), simply back off the breath, or slow down the rhythm, until the extra oxygen has been absorbed and the lightheadedness or tetany sensations go away. This is not harmful. Sometimes one has to just get used to having lots more oxygen.

As you do this breath, visualize an oval-shaped breath, in the belly: the inhale curves into the exhale; the exhale curves into the inhale. If you drift off, that's okay. Simply resume the breathing when you notice you've drifted off. Don't have any expectations or goals; don't worry about doing it "correctly." Just breathe.

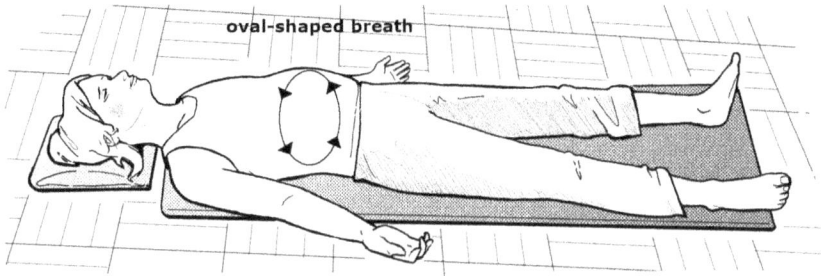

oval-shaped breath

You can practice belly breathing throughout the day, when you are sitting or lying down, or when you're just standing still. It will take away your stress, refresh you, give you energy and enable your body to heal naturally.

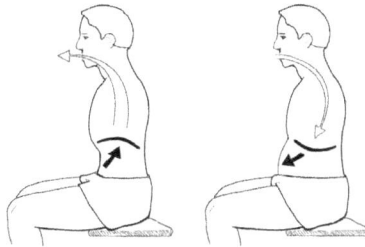

Sitting down

CHEST BREATH: After you're comfortable with the belly breath, and very relaxed, you can try the chest breath. To begin, inhale, pulling the diaphragm up, making a cave under the bottom of your rib cage.

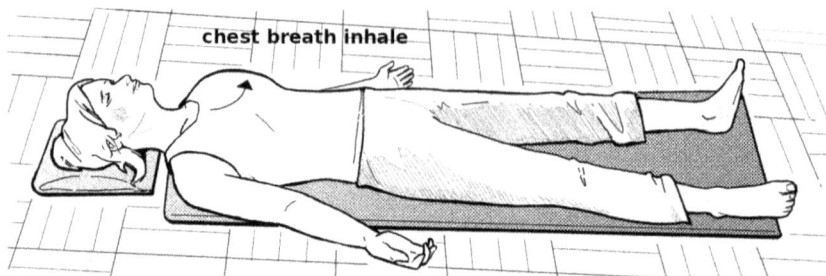

chest breath inhale

Now practice connecting the inhale to the exhale, and the exhale to the inhale. Visualize the air coming in at the breastbone, moving up the back of the spine, curving around at the top of the skull, then exhaling out through the nose, and the air comes in again at the breastbone. The inhale curves into the exhale; the exhale curves into the inhale. This is another oval-shaped breath, in medium-speed waltz rhythm: in-two-three; out-two-three.

Linger a bit on the curve at the top of the breath, just as the inhale is curving into the exhale. On the inhale, expand the rib cage to the front, the back and the sides.

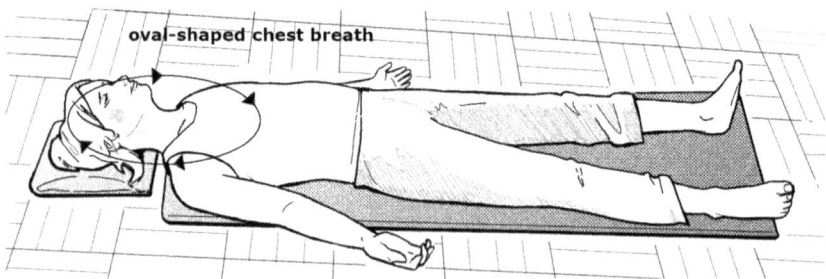

oval-shaped chest breath

This requires some muscular effort that you may not be used to, but as you practice, your muscles will get stronger and it will come easily.

Of course, the actual breath doesn't follow this oval shape, up the spine and around the skull and in at the breastbone, but focusing on the oval-shape helps you do the exercise properly and it gives the mind something to focus on so you're not caught up in mental chatter. "Give the monkey-mind something to do," as the Eastern meditation teachers say.

If you drift off while doing the breathing, that's perfectly okay. Just resume the breath and rhythm when you notice you drifted off. If you fall asleep and have a little cat nap during your breathing session, that's okay too. It means you needed the sleep!

The breath will give you exactly what you need. It has its own profound intelligence. Don't be goal-oriented, don't try to be perfect, let go of any expectations. Just focus on the oval-shaped breathing, staying in the present.

Remember, don't ever force the breath. More speed, more intensity, is not necessarily better. Do not deliberately stimulate your breath effects with loud evocative music. Go gradually, so that the benefits of the breath can integrate, instead of you being taken into some altered state outside yourself, getting an unnatural high. It may be a "high," but you'll crash afterward. And too much too fast, before one has actually relaxed into the breath, can cause one to go into hyperventilation, which is not healthy and could cause fainting.

With practice, you'll become more flexible in your breathing, so you'll breathe fully and easily, without thinking about it. Your body will naturally breathe in the way that's appropriate for any situation –

belly breath, chest breath, or a complete breath (filling the belly, then the chest).

Additional notes:

All vertebrates respond to stressful situations by releasing hormones, such as adrenalin and glucocorticoids, which instantaneously increase the animal's heart rate and energy level.

Glucocorticoids (GC) are a class of steroid hormones that bind to the glucocorticoid receptor (GR), which is present in almost every animal cell.

GCs are part of the feedback mechanism in the immune system that turns immune activity (inflammation) down.

Note on hyperventilation syndrome: Typically an anxious person takes small, shallow breaths, using their shoulders rather than their diaphragm to move air in and out of their lungs. This style of breathing empties too much carbon dioxide out of the blood and upsets the body's balance of gases. If they panic and start breathing faster, they can get into or hyperventilation, which causes even more anxiety and exacerbates physical symptoms of stress, including:

- Chest tightness

- Constant fatigue

- Faintness and lightheadedness

- Feelings of panic

- Headaches

- Heart palpitations

- Insomnia

- Muscular aches, twitches or stiffness

- Tingling, numb and cold hands and face.

BIBLIOGRAPHY

AFL-CIO. "Exporting America," www.aflcio.org/issues/jobseconomy/export-ingamerica/outsourcing_problems.cfm (accessed 11 August, 2011).

Alperovitz, Gar. "The New-economy movement: A growing group of activists and socially responsible companies are rethinking business as usual," *The Nation,* June 13, 2011. www.thenation.com/article/160949/new-economy-movement.

_____ "Neither Revolution Nor Reform: A New Strategy for the Left," *Dissent*, Fall 2011, http://dissentmagazine.org/article/?article=4056

American Psychiatric Association. *Diagnostic and Statistical Manual of Mental Disorders,* Fourth edition Text Revision (DSM-IV-TR) Washington D.C. 2000 pages 645–650.

Ariely, Dan. *Predictably Irrational: The Hidden Forces That Shape Our Decisions.* New York: Harper Perennial, 2010.

Bache, Christopher M. *Dark Night, Early Dawn: Steps to a deep Ecology of Mind.* Albany, New York: State University of New York Press, 2000.

Badgley, Catherine, J. Moghtader, J. Quintero, E. Zakem, M. J. Chappell, M. Jahi, K. Avilés-Vázquez, A. Samulon, and I. Perfecto. Organic agriculture and the global food supply. *Renewable Agriculture and Food Systems,* 22, 2007. pp 86-108.

Bearden, Tom. "Toward a New Electromagnetis, Part III: Clarifying the Vector Concept. 1983.www.cheniere.org/books/part3/implications.htm.

Bernstein, Jared and Lawrence Emishel. "Economy's Gains Fail to Reach Most Workers' Paychecks," EPI Briefing Paper, Economic Policy Institute, September 3, 2007. www.epi.org/page/-/old/briefingpapers/195/bp195.pdf.

Block, Ernst. *The Utopian Function of Art and Literature.* ed. J. Zipes and F. Mecklenburg Cambridge, Mass: MIT Press, 1988.

Braverman, Harry. *Labor and Monopoly Capital*, especially Chapter 4, "Scientific Management." New York: Monthly Review Press, 1998.

Board of Governors of the Federal Reserve System. "Factors Affecting Reserve Balances," Federal Reserve Statistical Release, October 13, 2011. www.federalreserve.gov/releases/h41/Current/.

Bohm, David, and Basil J. Hiley. *The Undivided Universe: An Ontological Interpretation of Quantum Theory.* New York: Routledge, 1995.

Borysenko, Joan. "Breathing, relaxation response," in *Minding the Body, Mending the Mind.* New York: Bantam New Age Books, 1988.

Buxton, Nick. "The Law of Mother Earth: Behind Bolivia's Historic Bill," *Yes Magazine*, April 22, 2011.www.yesmagazine.org/planet/the-law-of-mother-earth-behind-bolivias-historic-bill.

Byrd, Eldon, PhD. "High Voltage: The Megabrain Bioelectric Interviews," *Megabrain Report*, Vol.1 no.1, Edited by Michael Hutchison, 1991. http://preterhuman.net/texts/thought_and_writing/mind_control/brn-hv.txt (accessed 15 September 2011).

CNN Money. "CEOs earn 343 times more than typical workers." http://money.cnn.com/2011/04/19/news/economy/ceo_pay/index.htm (accessed 20 April 2011).

Dispenza, Joe. *Evolve Your Brain: The Science of Changing Your Mind.* Deerfield Beach, Florida: Health Communications Inc., 2007.

Dylan, Bob. "Bringing It All Back Home," audio recording. Coxsackie, NY: Sundazed Music Inc., 1965.

Easton and Guddat. *Writings of the Young Marx on Philosophy and Society*, "Money and Alienated Man." Indianapolis, IN: Hacket Publishing, 1972.

"Ecovillages." http://directory.ic.org/records/ecovillages.php. (accessed 6 October 2011).

Elgin, Duane. "A Garden of Simplicity Is Growing In the World," 2007. www.duaneelgin.com/articles/ garden-of-simplicity/ (accessed 8 August 2011).

"Equal Exchange." www.equalexchange.coop/farmer-partners. (accessed 5 October 2011.

Eriksson, P.S., et. al. "Neurogenesis in the Adult Human Hippocampus." *Nature Medicine*, 4(11). November 1998: 1313-7.

Freud, Sigmund. *An Outline of Psychoanalysis.* Translated by James Strachey. New York: Norton, 1940.

_____. *The Ego and the Id.* New York: W. W. Norton and Co. 1923.

Fuentes, Federico. "Bolivia: Amazon protest – development before environment?" http://boliviarising.blogspot.com/2011/09/bolivia-amazon-protest-development.html. (accessed 9 September 2011.

Gendlin, Eugene, PhD. *Focusing.* New York: Bantam Books (Random House), 1981.

Ghiselin, Brewster. *The Creative Process: Reflections on the Invention in the Arts and Science.* Berkeley: University of California Press, 1985.

"Glass-Steagall Act." Wikipedia. http://en.wikipedia.org/wiki/Glass-Steagall_Act. 5 November, 2011.

Godman, David, ed. Be as You Are: The Teachings of Sri Ramana Maharshi. New York: Arkana (Penguin), 1985.

Greene, Brian. *The Elegant Universe: Superstrings, Hidden Dimensions, and the Quest for the Ultimate Theory.* New York: Vintage Books, 1999.

Greer, Steven M., M.D. "Disclosure Project Briefing." www.disclosureproject.org/access/docs/pdf/DisclosureProjectBriefingDocument.pdf. 5 April 2001.

Halweil, Brian. "Can Organic Farming Feed Us All?" April 15, 2006, www.worldwatch.org/node/4060.

Hiltzik, Michael. "Taking Stock of CEO Pay." *Los Angeles Times.* May 10, 1996.

Ho, Mae Wan, Dr. "GMO versus Organics: Thirty years of GMOs are more than enough," ISIS Report, April 6, 2006, www.i-sis.org.uk/banGMOsNow.php.

_____. S. Burcher, L.C. Lim, et al. "Food Futures Now, Organic, Sustain-able, Fossil Fuel Free," ISIS and TWN, London, 2008. pdf p. 41, www.i-sis.org.uk/foodFutures.php.

_____. "GM-free organic agriculture to feed the world: International panel of 400 agricultural scientists call for fundamental change in farming practice." *Science in Society* 38, April 2008, www.i-sis.org.uk/GMFreeOrganicAgriculture.php.

_____. "The Case Against GM Crops and for Organic Sustainable Agriculture." Dr. Mae-Wan Ho Invited Workshop Presentation at National Justice and Peace Conference, 16-18 July 2010. ISIS Report 19/07/10. Swanick, UK, www.i-sis.org.uk/TheCaseAgainstGMCrops.php.

Hudson, Prof. Michael. "The Debt Ceiling Set For Progressive Repealing." http://michael-hudson.com/2011/07/debt-ceiling-for-progressive-repealing. 27 July 2011.

Jacoby, Russell. *Picture Imperfect: Utopian Thought for an Anti-Utopian Age.* New York: Columbia University Press, 2007.

Kempermann, G. and F.H. Gage. "New Nerve Cells for the Adult Brain." *Scientific American.* May 1999: 280(5): 48-53.

Krugman, Paul. "The Rich, The Right, and the Facts." *The American Prospect,* September 1, 1992, http://prospect.org/cs/articles?articleId=5232. 1

LaViolette, Paul A. *Subquantum Kinetics: A Systems Approach to Physics and Cosmology.* Niskayuna, New York: Starlane Publications, 2010.

_____. "Subquantum Kinetics Predictions and their Subsequent Verification," www.etheric.com/LaViolette/Predict2.html (accessed 25 July 2011).

Levine, Dr. Peter. "Nature's Lessons in Healing Trauma." Available at: www.traumahealing.com/somatic-experiencing/reference-healing-trauma-lessons-from-nature.pdf. 1996. (accessed16 September 2011).

_____. "The Body as Healer: A Revisioning of Trauma and Anxiety." unpublished paper. Boulder, CO: Foundation of Human Enrichment, 1996, www.traumahealing.com/somatic-experiencing/reference-trauma-and-anxiety-giving-the-body-its-due.pdf (accessed 16 September 2011).

_____. *Waking the Tiger.* Berkeley, CA: North Atlantic Books, 1997.

_____. "An Interview with Peter Levine, PhD," (interviewers Victor Yalom and Marie-Helene Yalom) April, 2010, www.psychotherapy.net/interview/interview-peter-levine#section-ptsd-medication

LoBuono, George. *Alien Mind: The Thought and Behavior of Extraterrestrials.* Davis, CA: QC Press, 2010.

Lukacs, Georg. *History and Class Consciousness.* Cambridge, Mass: MIT Press, 1971.

Magdoff, Fred, John Bellamy Foster. "What Every Environmentalist Needs to Know About Capitalism." Monthly Review, March 2010, Vol. 61:10, http://monthlyreview.org/2010/03/01/what-every-environmentalist-needs-to-know-about-capitalism#en11.

_____. *What Every Environmentalist Needs to Know About Capitalism.* New York: Monthly Review Press, 2011.

Marcuse, Herbert. in "History of Western Philosophy." www4.hmc.edu:8001/Humanities/Beckman/PhilNotes/marcuse.htm (accessed 5 April 2010).

_____. *One Dimensional Man: Studies in the Ideology of Advanced Psychology of Industrial Society.* Boston, Mass: Beacon Press, 1991.

_____. *The Aesthetic Dimension.* Boston, Mass: Beacon Press, 1977.

Marx, Karl. "Money and Alienated Man." in Easton and Guddat, *Writings of the Young Marx on Philosophy and Society*, Garden City, New York: Doubleday.

_____. *The German Ideology, Part I: Feuerbach,* "Opposition of the Materialist and Idealist Outlook." Amherst, NY: Prometheus Books, 1998, www.marxists.org/archive/marx/works/1845/german-ideology/ch01d.htm.

Maslow, Abraham. *Toward a Psychology of Being.* NY: John Wiley and Sons, 1968.

McChrystal, Karen, M.A. *The Creative Process.* unpublished masters thesis, San Francisco, 2008.

Meadows, Donella, Jorgen. Randers, and Dennis Meadows. *Limits to Growth – The 30 Year Update.* Claremont, NY: Chelsea Green Publishing Company, 2004.

"Mondragon Corporation." Wikipedia, http://en.wikipedia.org/wiki/Mondragon_Corporation#cite_note-0.

"National Employment Law Project," www.nelp.org/page/Justice/2011/-UnbalancedGrowthFeb2011.pdf?nocdn=1. www.bls.gov/oco/oco2003.htm.

Nelson, R. D., B. J. Dunne, Y. H. Dobyns, and R.G. Jahn. "Precognitive Remote Perception: Replication of Remote Viewing" (PDF). *Journal of Scientific Exploration* (Society for Scientific Exploration). 1996: 10 (1): 109–110. Available at: www.scientificexploration.org/journal/jse_10_1_nelson.pdf. 6 August 2011.

OECD. *"How's Life?: Measuring well-being."* OECD Publishing, doi: 10.1787/9789264121164-en (accessed 12 October 2011).

Puthoff, Harold and Russell Targ. "A Perceptual Channel for Information Transfer Over Kilometer Distances: Historical Perspective and Recent Research." *Proceedings of the IEEE.* March 1976: Vol. 64 No. 3

Radin, Dean, PhD. *Entangled Minds: Extrasensory Experiences in a Quantum Reality.* New York: Paraview Pocket Books (Simon and Schuster), 2006.

_____. "Testing nonlocal observation as a source of intuitive knowledge." *Explore.* Jan-Feb 2008: 4(1):25-35.

Rauscher, Dr. Elizabeth, and Russell Targ. "The Speed of Thought," *Journal of Scientific Exploration.* Society for Scientific Exploration. 2001: Vol. 15, No. 3, pp. 331–354, 2001 0892-3310/01. www.scientificexploration.org/ journal/jse_15_3_rauscher.pdf.

_____. "Investigation of a Complex Space-Time Metric to Describe Precognition of the Future," Frontiers of Time: Retrocausation – Experiment and Theory. AIP Conference Proceedings, Volume 863, pp. 121-146 (2006), www.espresearch.com/espgeneral/doc-SpeedOfThought.pdf.

Reed, Jack. *The Next Evolution: A Blueprint for Transforming the Planet,* Community Planet Foundation: Santa Barbara, CA, 2001. Excerpt reprinted with permission, courtesy of Jack Reed.

Rifkin, Jeremy. *The Third Industrial Revolution: How Lateral Power Is Transforming Energy, the Economy, and the World.* New York: Macmillan, 2011.

_____. "Beyond the Financial Crisis: Germany's Plan to Regrow the Global Economy." www.huffingtonpost.com/jeremy-rifkin/germany-euro-economy-_b_1028736.html.

Roberts, Paul Craig. "How Offshoring Has Destroyed the Economy," May 31, 2011, www.counterpunch.org/roberts05312011.html.

Rodale, Maria. "The Only Thing That Can Feed the World," Part 2. The Rodale Institute, Mar 27, 2011, www.care2.com/greenliving/the-only-thing-that-can-feed-the-world-part-2.html.

Rogers, Carl. *On Becoming a Person: A Therapist's View of Psychotherapy.* New York: Houghton Mifflin, 1961.

Schnabel, Jim. *The Secret History of America's Psychic Spies*, New York: Dell, 1997.

Seidel, George. *The Crisis of Creativity.* Indiana: University of Notre Dame Press, 1966.

Shan, Gao. "A Primary Quantum Model of Telepathy," The Scientists Work Team of Electro-Magnetic Wave Velocity. Chinese Institute of Electronics and Institute of Quantum Physics: Beijing, 2004.

Silberschatz, George, PhD. "How Patients Work On Their Plans and Test Their Therapists in Psychotherapy," 2008, http://sfprg.org/control_mastery/docs/Silberschatz2008.pdf.

Sirinathsinghji, Dr Eva. "Monsanto Defeated by Roundup Resistant Weeds," Institute of Science in Society, 2011, www.i-sis.org.uk/Monsanto_defeated_by_herbicide_resistant_superweeds.php.

Spence, Michael and Sandile Hlatshwayo. Report of the Council on Foreign Relations, "The Evolving Structure of the American Economy and the Employment Challenge," March 2011. www.cfr.org/industrial-policy/evolving-structure-american-economy-employment-challenge/p24366.

Suzuki, Daisetsu Teitaro. *Essays in Zen Buddhism*, Third Series. New Deli, India: Munshiram Manoharlal Publisers Pvt. Ltd., 1953.

Swan, Christopher. "Infrastructure Revolution," forthcoming, 2011.

_____. *Electric Water: The Emerging Revolution in Water and Energy.* British Columbia, Canada: New Society Publishers, 2007.

"Sweden Going Green." *Sydney Morning Herald.* June 23, 2007, www.smh.com.au/news/environment/going-green/2007/06/22/1182019367503.html.

"Sweden: How Clean is Your Economy?" Online Editor, New European Economy, Sept. 3, 2011. www.neweuropeaneconomy.com/Site_Content/Insight/Sweden_-_How_Clean_Is_Your_Economy?/.

Targ, Russell, and Jane Katra, Ph.D. "The Scientific and Spiritual Implications of Psychic Abilities," Palo Alto, CA, 2001, www.espresearch.com/espgeneral/doc-AT.shtml.

_____. *Limitless Mind.* Novato, CA: New World Library, 2004.

Treadwell, Benjamin V., Ph.D. "The Aging Brain: Why We Forget and What Might Help." *Juvenon Health Journal*, June 2011, http://juvenon.com/jhj/vol10no06w.htm.

Vidal, John. "Bolivia enshrines natural world's rights with equal status for Mother Earth" *The Guardian.* April 2011, www.guardian.co.uk/environment/2011/apr/10/bolivia-enshrines-natural-worlds-rights.

Weiss, Joseph, and Harold Sampson. *The Psychoanalytic Process: Theory,*

Clinical Observation and Empirical Research. The Mount Zion Psychotherapy Research Group, New York: The Guilford Press, 1986. More information available at http://sfprg.org/control_mastery/index. html#introduction.

Wolff, Richard D. "Deepening Economic Divisions" *Monthly Review magazine*, January 2011, http://mrzine.monthlyreview.org/2011/wolff170111. html.

_____. "Labor Movement?" http://rdwolff.com/content/labor-movement. December 24, 2009.

Wolin, Sheldon S. *Politics and Vision.* Princeton, New Jersey: Princeton University Press, 1960, 2004.

"World Population." Wikipedia, http://en.wikipedia.org/wiki/World_population (accessed 12 August 2011).

Zamyatin, Yevgeny. *We.* London: UK: Penguin Twentieth Century Classics, 1993 (originally published in 1921; first English translation: Dutton: New York, 1924).

www.ingramcontent.com/pod-product-compliance
Lightning Source LLC
Chambersburg PA
CBHW051951090426
42741CB00008B/1352